THE POWER IN CAKEWALK SONAR

quick**PRO**
guides

THE POWER IN CAKEWALK SONAR

William Edstrom, Jr.

Hal Leonard Books
An Imprint of Hal Leonard Corporation

Published in 2013 by Hal Leonard Books
An Imprint of Hal Leonard Corporation
7777 West Bluemound Road
Milwaukee, WI 53213

Trade Book Division Editorial Offices
33 Plymouth St., Montclair, NJ 07042

Printed in the United States of America

Book design by Adam Fulrath
Book composition by Kristina Rolander

Library of Congress Cataloging-in-Publication Data

Edstrom, William, Jr.
 The power in Cakewalk SONAR / William Edstrom.
     pages cm. -- (Quick pro guides)
 Includes bibliographical references and index.
 1. Sonar (Computer file) 2. Digital audio editors. I. Title.
 ML74.4.S66E37 2013
 781.3'4536--dc23
                                        2013021719

ISBN 9781476806013

www.halleonardbooks.com

CONTENTS

Introduction

PART I: GETTING STARTED

Chapter 1

Chapter 2

Chapter 3

Chapter 4

Chapter 5

Chapter 6

Chapter 7

Chapter 8

Chapter 9

PART II: RECORDING AND EDITING

Chapter 10

Chapter 11

Chapter 12

Recording with Soft Synths... **103**

Chapter 13

Editing MIDI **109**

Chapter 14

PART III: EFFECTS & MIXING

Chapter 15

Chapter 16

Chapter 17

PREFACE

With this book, my goal is to help you learn the most straightforward path to making music with SONAR. As a long-term Cakewalk SONAR user, I enjoyed putting together this guide, which includes all the core features along with powerful new workflows from the latest version.

Every chapter presents the most up-to-date approach to working in SONAR. I will show you how to simplify the appearance of SONAR so you can focus more on music and a little less on technology. SONAR is an amazing tool for recording and creating carefully edited and mixed professional records. It is also functions as a scratch pad for creative sound exploration.

ACKNOWLEDGMENTS

Thanks to the team at Cakewalk for continuing to improve SONAR version after version. Thank you specifically to Marcus for helping me find the right person to answer my questions at Cakewalk. Thanks to Roland USA for loaning me an Octa-Capture interface while writing the book.

Thank you to SONAR power user Jeff Pettit, who proofread the manuscript and gave me numerous suggestions that made the book much better. Thanks to Mana Mostatabi, who assisted me with proofreading, editing, and indexing. Special thanks to singer/songwriter Letta, who gave me permission to use her song for the book and DVD.

Thank you to the team at Hal Leonard Books: Bill Gibson, my developmental editor, for encouragement and patience; Matt Cerullo, the project editor, who saw the book through to the end; and Iris Bass. the copyeditor, for greatly improving the readability of the text.

Thank you to my siblings Cindy, Art, and Eric for ongoing encouragement to live an amazing life. Thanks to my young son, Toma, for being a continuous source of love and entertainment. Thanks to my elder son, Andrew, for inspiring with a constant stream of big ideas. Special thanks to my wife, Mari, who helped script the formatting of the manuscript and created all the QR codes, but mostly for her endless support and love.

THE POWER IN CAKEWALK SONAR

INTRODUCTION

This book tours the power in SONAR. Because the book is presented as a Quick Pro Guide, I focus on explaining SONAR in as clear and direct terms as possible. Because of the complexity of the program, it is not possible to be completely comprehensive. I present the core workflows—recording, editing, mixing, and releasing—of music production as the framework to introduce SONAR features. The videos on the DVD-ROM bring some of the topics to life and introduce a few additional topics that didn't fit into the book.

Because a computer is the center of all this, I will detail some setup and technology issues that you must deal with before you hit Record. I also offer some music production tips and techniques along the way. In many cases, I point to other online resources that can help fill in some of the fundamentals if you are new to computer-based music production.

SONAR

Cakewalk holds a trademark for SONAR (in all caps) for use in branding its DAW software. To respect the trademark and branding, I will use SONAR throughout the book.

Figures

To make topics as clear as possible, the book is liberally illustrated with screenshots and callouts. All figures in the book are placed near their relevant text. Most of those figures are screenshot images taken directly from my SONAR projects.

Menus

The following format will be used whenever SONAR menu items are discussed: Process > Apply Effect > Reverse. This path format should be easy to relate to the corresponding menu selection.

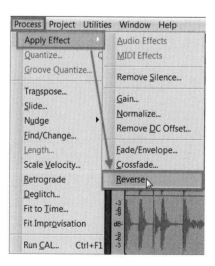

Figure I-1. Process > Apply Effect > Reverse

QR Codes

Links to websites are provided by convenient QR codes. This makes it easy to use a QR code reader app on your mobile device to get to the page. If you want to type in URLs, you will find them cross-referenced to the figure numbers in the appendix.

PART I: GETTING STARTED

Chapter 1
THE HISTORY OF CAKEWALK SONAR

Starting with version X1, Cakewalk modernized the SONAR user interface and named it Skylight. This was a risky move and some longtime users didn't like the change at first. I was also skeptical when I first saw demos of Skylight. But as I started to work with Skylight, I quickly experienced the advantages. Skylight, the ProChannel, and the improved Smart tool elevate SONAR to a new level of capability and efficiency. I think you will find that SONAR works as well on a modern laptop as it does on a dual-monitor desktop rig. SONAR has everything needed for music production, whether you are just getting started or are already a professional audio engineer.

Cakewalk has left older tools and plug-ins in place to make it easier for longtime users to continue working after upgrading. If you are a new user, you will quickly discover there are several ways to do any one thing. A full SONAR installation includes many generations of plug-in effects and Soft Synths that I will help you sort into those that are relevant and those that are dated. If you have projects built with older versions, it's helpful to have all the legacy technology available for your old projects. For new projects, you can choose from a wide array of the latest effects and instruments.

About SONAR

SONAR evolved from the DOS program Cakewalk. Back in the day, the company name was Twelve Tone Systems. Cakewalk was one of the first PC-based MIDI sequencers of the 1980s. By the mid-1990s, Cakewalk migrated to Windows and added digital audio recording. I've used Cakewalk software for parts of four decades! At first I was running racks of sound modules synced to tape or ADAT machines then later by recording audio and MIDI to Cakewalk Pro Audio as it developed in a complete music production system. Today, this type of system is called a digital audio workstation (DAW).

In the 2000s, Cakewalk Pro Audio was renamed SONAR and continued to adapt to the rapidly increasing power of processors and large, affordable hard drives. SONAR was one of the first DAWs to make the leap to 64-bit processing. This in turn allowed the use of large amounts of random-access memory (RAM) to run extremely large projects, including large orchestral Soft Synths instruments, natively. For most of this first decade, SONAR has been my main tool for music production, recording, mixing, and transferring audio from analog to digital systems.

With the start of new decade, Cakewalk made a bold move to update the SONAR user interface (UI) with the launch of X1. It took the SONAR user community time to adjust to the Skylight UI; and Cakewalk, a few incremental releases to stabilize the experience. As with many changes, we can now see that this major overhaul was worth it. SONAR X2 represents a fully realized Skylight interface that has been refined and extended to include dozens of workflow optimizations and powerful new effects.

Figure 1.1. SONAR's Skylight interface

Skylight brings together a deep feature set and a modern single-window interface designed for big-screen, high-resolution monitors. It is easy to focus on the Track view, Console view, or one of the other detailed edit views. You can open and close additional resources, such as the Browser pane, Inspector pane, Staff view, or Matrix view. There is also full support for dual-monitor setups that allow you to have, for example, the Track view on one screen and the console on the other.

Skylight also changes the way we work with tools. The Smart tool in X1 reduced the need to switch tools while editing. Since X2, the enhanced Smart tool almost eliminates any need to switch tools at all. This new way of working in SONAR is more efficient, easier to learn, and more pleasurable.

Undoubtedly, the most innovative feature of Skylight is the modular ProChannel, found in Console view and the Inspector pane. The ProChannel allows you to design a customized mixing console with compression, EQ, and other effects on every channel. Use the same ProChannel setup on every channel or customize them for different instruments and voices. The available third-party and optional ProChannel modules make this an exciting feature to explore during the course of this book.

Figure 1.2. ProChannel

Cakewalk and Roland's long relationship resulted in Cakewalk's becoming a part of Roland's extensive line of music production products. This has led to an exciting integration of Roland hardware with SONAR, which is one of its most unique advantages. For example, Cakewalk works seamlessly with the full range of Roland audio interfaces. While writing this book, I used the Roland Octa-Capture when working on many of the examples. I also use the Roland Tri-Capture as part of my mobile and voiceover setups.

When using SONAR with Roland's A-PRO keyboard controller line, ACT (active controller technology), enables deep integration of the hardware knobs, faders, and buttons with the software. This is an extremely powerful integration that even longtime SONAR users often overlook. A-PRO keyboards bring a hands-on feel to music production with SONAR at a very low cost.

Figure 1.3. Roland Octa-Capture

Figure 1.4. Roland A-500 PRO Keyboard

The V-Studio 700 brings you a pro-quality control surface that comes premapped to work with SONAR. Cakewalk has refined the integration to allow hands-on control of all ProChannel effects, the transport, the mix, the recording functions, and some nice long-throw faders. While I won't cover the V-Studio in this book, it is important to know that there is a full range of hardware available to take advantage of the power found in SONAR.

Although using Roland hardware with Cakewalk has certain conveniences, it is not a requirement. SONAR supports most audio interfaces that work with Windows. I have used SONAR successfully with interfaces and digital mixers from such companies as MOTU, PreSonus, Focusrite, and Sound Devices. I have also successfully used controllers from AKAI and M-Audio to play the SONAR Soft Synths.

Great gear can expand your creative options, improve sound quality, and allow you to work faster. However, to make great music, all you need is a two-channel audio interface, a microphone, headphones, a suitable computer, and Cakewalk SONAR.

Preferences

In SONAR, you configure most settings and options by using the Preferences dialog box, accessible under Files > Preferences or simply by using the keyboard shortcut P. Almost every chapter in the book refers to settings in this dialog box, so it is a good idea to learn how to open it and familiarize yourself with it as a whole. The Preferences dialog box has Basic and Advanced modes, which you can choose in the lower left. Basic mode hides some of the features. I just leave it set to Advanced.

Figure 1.5. The Preferences dialog box

Keyboard Shortcuts

Throughout the book, I point out important keyboard shortcuts. Keyboard shortcuts are shown with abbreviated modifier keys, such as Ctrl + C, Alt + F1, and Shift + F. Single-character modifiers, such as using P for preferences, are simply shown as capital letters. In many cases, the keyboard shortcut for an action will be shown in parenthesis in the description. As an example: To get ready to mix, first open Console view (Alt + 2) to access SONAR's virtual mixer.

For the most part, SONAR's default keyboard shortcuts are well thought out and effective. If you came from a different system, or if you just have a different way of working, then you can reassign them in the Preferences dialog box, as shown in Fig. 1.5. Notice you need to be in Advanced mode to see the Keyboard Shortcuts page.

Now that you have a bit of background, let's take a closer look at SONAR.

Chapter 2
COMPUTERS, WINDOWS, AND SONAR

You need a Windows computer to run SONAR. This chapter details recommendations and resources for selecting a computer that meets the required specifications to run SONAR. I will also explain how to install SONAR and configure Microsoft Windows for the best audio performance.

Computer Requirements

SONAR runs on Windows PCs and the computer requirements are fairly modest. Following are the official minimum requirements published by Cakewalk for SONAR X2:

- Windows 7 or Windows 8 (32- and 64-bit). XP and Vista are no longer officially supported.
- Intel Core 2 Duo E8200 2.67 GHz/AMD Phenom Quad Core 9750 2.4 GHz or higher
- 2 GB of RAM
- 1,280x800 minimum screen resolution
- 4.5 GB for minimal install, 20 GB recommended
- Broadband Internet connection for download

I suggest using a more powerful machine than the minimum spec. A good baseline machine is an Intel-based PC or laptop that has an i5 or i7 processor, 8 GB or more of RAM, and a 64-bit version of Windows 7. This will give you enough power for relatively large projects and enough RAM to load some big virtual instruments. Look for 7,200 rpm hard drives or SSDs (solid-state disks). Although SSDs are more expensive and a smaller storage capacity, they are faster and less susceptible to mechanical crashes. I have been enjoying very good performance by using an SSD for my Windows boot drive.

Installing SONAR

You can install SONAR from a DVD-ROM disk if you purchased the boxed retail package. If you purchased online, you can download the setup files from your account found in the Cakewalk Store. Either way, you need to set up your account in the Cakewalk Store to access updates.

Figure 2.1. Cakewalk store

> **Tip:** I highly recommend that you register your SONAR serial numbers and download the files even if you have the installation disks, as Cakewalk frequently updates SONAR and the disks are almost certainly out of date. You can find detailed installation instructions at the following address:

Figure 2.2. SONAR X2 installation
instructions link

Downloading the Setup Files

Setup comprises a number of files that you can see as soon as you access your account. Download all the files to one folder on your computer before running any of them. I store all my setup files for downloaded software in the Downloads folder and organize it by vendor name and product. In this case, I put the setup files in the Downloads/Cakewalk/SONAR X2 folder.

Some files will come in a compressed Zip format, including the sound libraries for the Dimension Pro virtual instrument. Right-click each Zip file and select Extract All to unzip them. After you have extracted the files, you can delete the original Zip files.

If you want information on updates and known issues, double-click "01_Read_This_First," which will extract the Readme file in several languages. To actually install SONAR, double-click the file named "02_SONAR_X2_Producer.part," which will extract the setup binary files. This takes several minutes, so you might want to take a break at this point! When the extraction is finished, the installer will start and walk you through the process step by step.

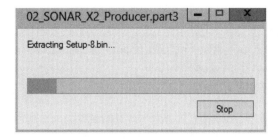

Figure 2.3. Time to take a break!

I tried installing SONAR X2 in different ways while writing this book. At first, I customized the location of some of the folders, including the location of VST plug-ins, but concluded after much experimentation that the defaults work best for most of the installation prompts.

Choosing the 32-Bit or 64-Bit Version

One of the first installation dialog boxes asks you to select between the 32-bit and the 64-bit version. If you have a modern computer running a 64-bit version of Windows and have more than 4 GB of RAM, then select the 64-bit version. If your computer is older, or you have 4 GB or less of RAM, then choose the 32-bit version. On my computers, I always use the 64-bit version.

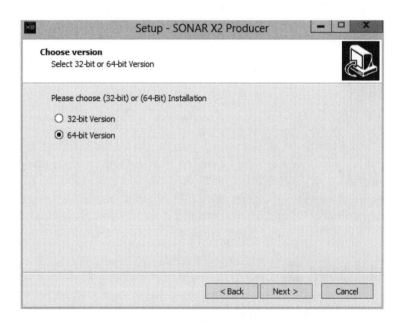

Figure 2.4. Choose version during installation.

Changing the Location of SONAR Project Folders

It is a good idea to record and edit SONAR projects on a separate hard drive. Most PCs have one big C drive that holds Windows, as well as programs, documents, and media. For the past fifteen years, I have received and given this same advice: load Windows and programs on the C drive and keep all your working data on a second drive. If you have a desktop computer, consider adding a second high-speed drive for recording. If you are using a laptop, think about adding a high-speed external drive. Digital recording uses a lot of disk space, but this is not a problem for modern hard drives, as they come with huge amounts of high-speed storage.

It is indeed possible to record substantial projects on a single drive system. I do most of my SONAR work on a laptop computer that has a single 512 GB SSD drive. I use a quad-core i7 laptop with 16 GB of RAM, running Windows 7 Home Premium that rarely has any trouble keeping up with large projects. Modern multicore computers and laptops are brilliantly speedy.

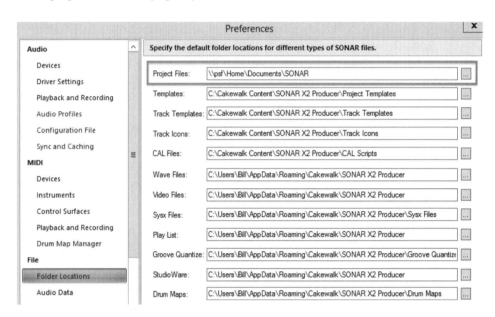

Figure 2.5. Setting the location of project files

To change the default location for project files, open the Preferences dialog box (keyboard shortcut P) and navigate to Folder Locations. If I am using a single drive system, I like to keep projects in a folder titled "SONAR" in my Documents folder. If I am using a separate hard drive, I create a folder named "D:\SONAR" and set this as the default. If you already have projects created, you can just drag and copy them over to the new folder.

Using Windows 8

If you want the most stable and best-supported experience with SONAR, it is advisable to use Windows 7 64-bit. SONAR X2 does support Windows 8 since the X2a release. The most interesting thing about SONAR on Windows 8 is how it works with multitouch monitors. I tested this firsthand by connecting a Dell 23-inch multitouch LED monitor to my DAW computer. After connecting the monitor, connect a separate USB3 cable from the computer to the monitor to access the touch screen. In this case, USB3 is required.

This setup supports up to eight simultaneous touches that open up some interesting features in SONAR:

- In Console view, adjust up to eight faders, using your fingers at the same time.
- In Track view, zoom in and out of tracks, using pinch gestures.

- In Matrix view, launch loop cells and columns—even several at once.
- Position the now time.
- Mute, solo, and unmute tracks.

There is a thirty-millisecond delay for touch screen moves, so the faders don't move instantly. Keep an eye on this technology as better solutions emerge over the next few years, as this could be a key element to interacting with SONAR in the future. If you like to be an early adopter, get started right now.

Keep in mind that Windows 8 has a different interface than the previous version of Windows. I used Windows 8 during the writing of this book and it worked well with SONAR. I used the open-source Classic Shell to make Windows 8 work mostly like Windows 7. Most SONAR users will probably want to do the same thing. With all that talk about Windows 8, I still stand by my initial recommendation that Windows 7 64-bit is probably the best choice as a platform for SONAR.

Optimizing Windows

SONAR has a huge user base, running on just about every imaginable brand of computer. Certainly, many are successfully running on off-the-shelf Dell, HP, or Lenovo machines. However, many have trouble using mass-market computers because they are not optimized for high-bandwidth audio. The issues usually surface as audio dropouts, crackles, or program crashes.

If you are using a general-purpose PC and are having problems, you will need to do some optimization to streamline the system. Optimization usually involves uninstalling unneeded software, tweaking Windows options, and potentially disabling Wi-Fi and virus scanning while running SONAR. Here are some popular guides for optimizing Windows for digital audio:

Figure 2.6. Focusrite Windows optimization QR Code

Figure 2.7. Windows optimization Cakewalk forum QR Code

Figure 2.8. Sweetwater Windows optimization tips QR Code

Selecting a SONAR Computer

Building a stable Windows platform for recording can become an obsession, or even for some, an all-consuming hobby. You can put together a powerful SONAR machine from parts and may even be able to save a few dollars in the process. Here are some resources for selecting parts and getting support for rolling your own DAW PC:

Figure 2.9. Gearslutz DAW building thread QR Code

Figure 2.10. Tom's hardware DAW building thread QR Code

If you want to avoid the hassle of optimization or building your own system, consider buying a purpose-built DAW computer from a reputable company. Builders put together tested components and set up Windows in a way that is optimized for digital audio without all the unnecessary software that bogs down off-the-shelf computers.

Following is a list of the top suppliers of prebuilt DAW computers in the United States:

- Rain Computers (Figure 2.11)
- PCAudioLabs (Figure 2.12)
- Purrrfect Audio (Figure 2.13)
- ADK Pro Audio (Figure 2.14)
- Sweetwater Sound (Figure 2.15)

Figure 2.11. Rain Computers QR Code

Figure 2.12. PCAudioLabs QR Code

Figure 2.13. Purrrfect Audio QR Code

Figure 2.14. ADK Pro Audio QR Code

Figure 2.15. Sweetwater Sound QR Code

Computer Management and Backup

Whatever computer you decide to use, make sure to have a backup plan. I use a program called GoodSync to sync my SONAR projects to a USB hard drive at the end of each session.

Figure 2.16. Siber Systems GoodSync

I also create a disk image once a month or before any major Windows or SONAR upgrade. It is important to give yourself a plan B so you can roll back if something goes wrong. There are lots of disk imaging solutions; the one I currently use is called EaseUS Todo Backup Free.

Figure 2.17. EaseUS Todo Backup Free

I suggest setting up SONAR with a few essential Windows tools that can benefit any project studio. First is Dropbox, which allows you to put files in a special folder on your computer and share them with multiple computers and people. I keep Dropbox on my desktop and could not imagine running my studio without it.

Figure 2.18. Dropbox

Consider 1Password for password management. 1Password syncs between Mac, Windows, and iOS devices by using Dropbox. It keeps track of all your online passwords, so you can easily log into Gmail, Cakewalk Store, and all of the hundreds of websites you rely on daily. The Dropbox sync keeps a master file of passwords and fills them in automatically from a master password—you only need to remember one!

Figure 2.19. Agilebits 1Password

For virus scanning, I stay away from the expensive and bulky commercial packages and use the free, basic offering from Microsoft called Security Essentials. You can disable it during recording if it causes trouble. If you don't already have the virus scanner, you can download it for free (Figure 2.20).

Figure 2.20. Microsoft Security
Essentials

Now with SONAR installed and your computer tuned for audio, let's get sound going
in and out of SONAR.

Chapter 3
AUDIO DEVICE SETUP

SONAR software is the heart of your computer-based studio. However, to have a functioning digital recording studio, you need an audio interface. Audio interfaces provide the following essential functions to your SONAR setup:

- Connection to your monitor speakers and control room level
- Connection for headphones and headphone level
- Inputs for microphones and guitars
- Low-latency monitoring while recording

Figure 3.1. Audio interface functions

The aforementioned four items are the essential functions the device provides. How the unit is connected, its number of mic inputs, and other features can vary dramatically, with prices ranging from under a hundred to thousands of dollars. You may already have an audio interface, but if you don't, you will find hundreds of choices, with new models released nearly every month.

Modern audio interfaces usually connect to your computer via USB or Firewire. Because most laptop computers no longer include Firewire connectivity, USB interfaces are the most common. Manufacturers are also starting to offer Thunderbolt interfaces, for which I expect to see more and more choices emerge.

Fortunately, the setup is similar regardless of which interface brand or model you use. The following sections detail the steps to get your audio interface connected and tested for playback. Because the Roland Octa-Capture is one of the most popular interfaces for SONAR, I will use that device in the examples.

Installing Audio Device Drivers

Audio interfaces have used many technologies over the years to interface with Microsoft Windows. Fortunately for Windows users, ASIO (usually pronounced Ah-zee-oh) has emerged as the industry standard. ASIO, short for "audio stream input/output," provides an efficient, high-fidelity interface between SONAR and your external hardware. SONAR supports several types of Windows drivers, but most often you will want to choose ASIO as the driver type. I will show you how to do that shortly.

Your audio interface will come with ASIO driver software you need to install before using it with such recording apps as SONAR. Manufacturers always include a driver disk with the hardware, but the boxed disks are almost always out of date. Go to the manufacturer's website and download the latest drivers. You can find the latest drivers for Roland gear at the website noted in Fig. 3.2.

Figure 3.2. Roland drivers web link

Don't connect the interface to your computer yet. Make sure SONAR is not running. Install the driver software from the downloaded file. The driver installer will walk you through installing and connecting the interface. Sometimes a newly installed driver will also prompt you to update the hardware firmware.

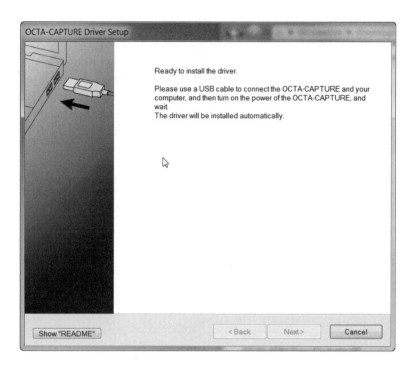

Figure 3.3. Octa-Capture driver installation

Setting Audio Device Preferences

After installing the driver software, open SONAR. If the Quick Start dialog box comes up, just close it. Open the Preferences dialog box (P) and navigate to the Playback and Recording page under the Audio section. On this page, make sure ASIO is selected for Drive Mode and click Apply.

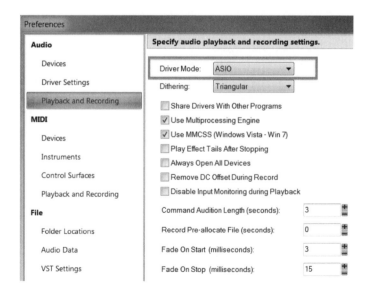

Figure 3.4. Playback and recording preferences

Next, select the Devices page and set up your inputs and outputs. By default, all hardware outputs will be mapped to SONAR. Inputs and outputs are already prenamed by the hardware manufacturer. These names tend to be long and technical, but you can rename them with what SONAR calls "friendly names." Simply double-click the name to edit it. I like to use friendly names that match the sticker labels I attach to my hardware to make it as clear as possible when working in the software. I also tend to deselect any I/O not connected to anything. When you are happy with the I/O setup and friendly names, click Apply.

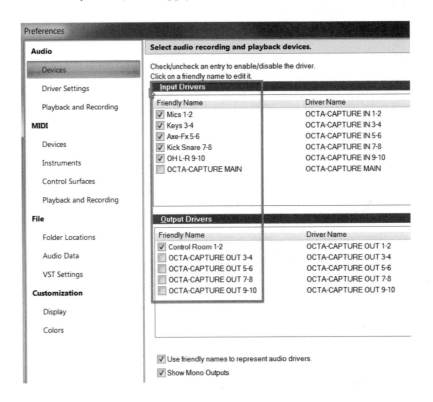

Figure 3.5. Devices preferences

Now select the Driver Settings page and verify that your device is set as both the Playback Timing Master and the Recording Timing Master. If it is not, make those changes and click Apply. At this point, your interface is configured and ready to rock!

Figure 3.6 Driver Settings

Before we leave the Driver Settings page, I want to point out the button labeled "ASIO Panel." Clicking this button will open the audio interface manufacturer's settings program, where you can fine-tune buffers to affect system latency. This will be important when we get into recording with virtual instruments and guitar amp simulators.

Latency is the time you give SONAR to "think" between when you play and when you hear back the notes. If you play the keyboard and the sound is coming out a half-second later, it can throw off your timing. However, if you lower latency to next to nothing, SONAR will not have time to do the necessary computations for a clean output. Using SONAR is always a balance of giving the software more time to think and giving you minimal timing latency.

The ASIO Panel is where you adjust latency. If you don't see this directly after clicking the ASIO Panel button, you will find it under Driver Settings on the Octa-Capture Control Panel. The format of this screen will vary by manufacturer, but in all cases you can set the buffer size to affect latency. For Roland hardware, the buffer setting is a horizontal slider that defaults to 6, which correlates to a buffer size of 256 samples. This is a good starting point for most systems. If you don't get clean playback, increase the number. If you feel as if there is too much delay with the virtual instruments, then lower it.

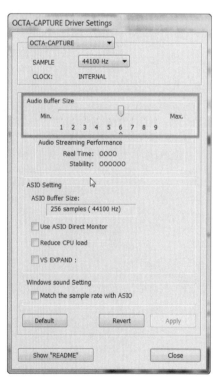

Figure 3.7. Octa-Capture Driver Settings

Testing Playback

The final step is to make sure you can hear playback. Load one of the demo songs or drag any audio from your computer to the Track view and hit the space bar. You will need to have headphones or have your speakers on and the volume on the interface turned up, to hear playback. Playback is done simply by hitting the space bar or the

Play button on the SONAR Control Bar.

If you hear nothing, then check that you have the correct output select on the Master in the Console. Here is how to do that:

1. Open the Console view (Views > Console view).
2. Find the Master channel at the far right.
3. In the In/Out section, verify that the correct output is selected.

Note: If you don't see the In/Out section, you can enable that in the Console view menu under Modules In/Out.

Using Built-in Sound

For professional results, use an external audio interface with ASIO drivers. But if you are in a coffee shop or on an airplane and just want to hook up headphones

Figure 3.8. Select the Master Channel Output

for editing, change the Driver Mode on the Playback and Recording page. Usually, changing it to MME (32-bit) will be enough to get playback happening. Just make sure to change it back to ASIO when you are again connected to your audio interface.

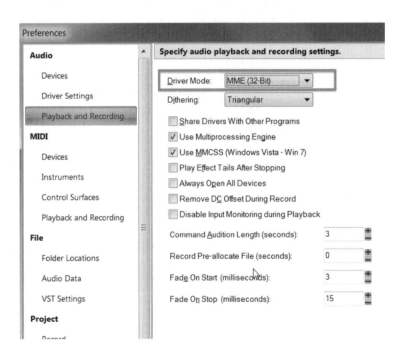

Figure 3.9. Setting the Driver Mode to MME (32-bit)

With audio flowing from your computer, you can now move on to the MIDI setup.

Chapter 4
MIDI Device Setup

To play virtual instruments (Soft Synths) in SONAR, you need an external keyboard or drum pad controller. Most modern controllers connect via USB, like any other computer peripheral. MIDI is the name of a protocol that transmits notes you play on the controller to such software as SONAR. If you route the MIDI data to a Soft Synth, then the notes you play come to life as instrument sounds. SONAR includes a nice selection of great-sounding Soft Synths and supports most third-party plug-in instruments as well.

Many modern keyboards have extra features, such as knobs, faders, buttons, and transport controls. We will get into that later in this book, but first I will go over the basics of configuring a MIDI keyboard controller.

There are dozens of MIDI keyboard controllers on the market. Most of them will work just fine with SONAR. For this section, I will walk through the setup for a Roland A-500Pro. This is a very nice match for SONAR and has some extra integration that makes it a good example of a typical MIDI setup.

Basic MIDI Keyboard Controller Installation

Some modern keyboards don't require special drivers, so if you have a simple keyboard, this step may not be necessary. The only way to really know is visit the manufacturer's website and look for drivers. If none is available, then the keyboard will probably connect without special drivers. The AKAI LPK25, for example, works fine without any additional drivers. For such types of keyboards, just connect the USB cable, restart SONAR, and load the Preferences dialog box (P). Navigate to the Devices page in the MIDI section. To complete the setup, select the device name (in this case, LPK25) in both the input and output sections.

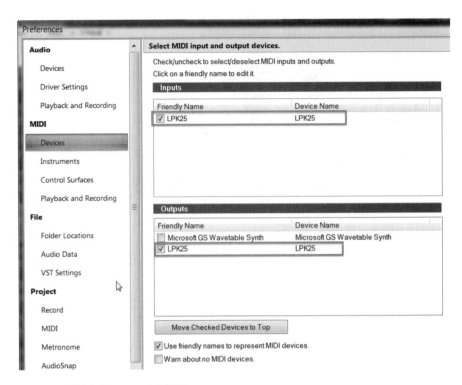

Figure 4.1. MIDI devices setup for LPK25

Advanced MIDI Keyboard Controller Installation

More capable MIDI keyboard controllers require special drivers. This is true of the Roland A-500Pro and the entire A-Pro line of keyboards. For Roland keyboards, you can find driver downloads here:

Figure 4.2. Roland keyboard drivers GQ Code

Install the drivers then connect the keyboard to your computer, using a USB cable. As before, press P to load the Preferences dialog box and navigate to the Device page in the MIDI section (Figure 4.3). A-Pro keyboards are presented in SONAR as three different input ports and two output ports.

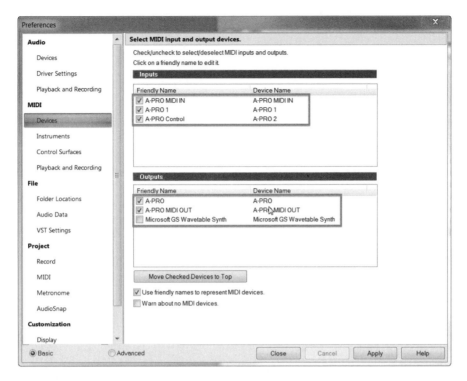

Figure 4.3. MIDI Device page in Preferences

The easiest way to configure this is to select all the inputs and outputs with a name matching your controller. However, it is helpful to understand what each port actually does. Here is a breakdown that uses the A-500Pro as our example.

A-Pro MIDI IN. This port is for MIDI cable connections to the actual five-pin jack on the side of the keyboard. If you don't plan to connect anything via a MIDI cable, you can leave this unchecked.

A-Pro 1. This is the input port that transmits MIDI notes from the keyboard to SONAR. This one must be checked to be able to play Soft Synths from the keyboard.

A-Pro 2. In Fig. 4.3, I renamed the A-Pro 2 port to "A-Pro Control." This input port transmits the data from the knobs, faders, and transport buttons of the keyboard controller to SONAR. Read further and also see Chapter 21 to learn how to set up ACT (Active Controller Technology) to control all kinds of parameters in SONAR.

A-Pro. This output is used to transmit data back to the keyboard. This is usually used to restore backups for the keyboard settings. Usually you will want to enable this device.

A-Pro MIDI OUT. This is the output to the five-pin MIDI out port on the back of the keyboard. These usually connect to older sound modules and keyboards with internal sounds that cannot connect via USB. If you don't plan to use external MIDI sound modules, you can leave this unchecked.

Although I am using the A-500Pro as an example, other models and brands of keyboards have a similar setup. Make sure to click Apply before leaving the Preferences dialog box to ensure the changes stick.

Chapter **5**

NAVIGATING SKYLIGHT

Y ou build songs in SONAR by using what Cakewalk has dubbed Skylight—a collection of panes and views organized into a single window. The Skylight user interface (UI) was introduced with X1 and has been further refined since.

Figure 5.1. The Skylight user interface

The Parts of Skylight

Skylight takes full advantage of modern widescreen displays and multiple display setups. It also adapts well to laptop use. You can move most of the elements to other parts of the window or float views into separate windows.

The Skylight UI is made up of these parts:

Control Bar. The Control Bar contains quick access to editing tools, transport controls, and important status information about your project. It is made up of thirteen modules that can be turned on or off from a simple right-click menu. The essential Control Bar modules are Tools, Snap, Transport, Loop, and Mix. Grab any blank space on the Control Bar to pull it free and use it as floating palette. Use keyboard shortcut C to hide or show the Control Bar.

Figure 5.2. The Control Bar

Track View. As long as you have a project open, Track view is front and center. The left side is called the Track pane and the right side is called the Clips pane. The Track pane is essentially a list of track headers (called track strips). The Clips pane holds all your project's audio and MIDI clips. Track view has its own set of menus along the top edge, which give you lots of additional options for working within this view.

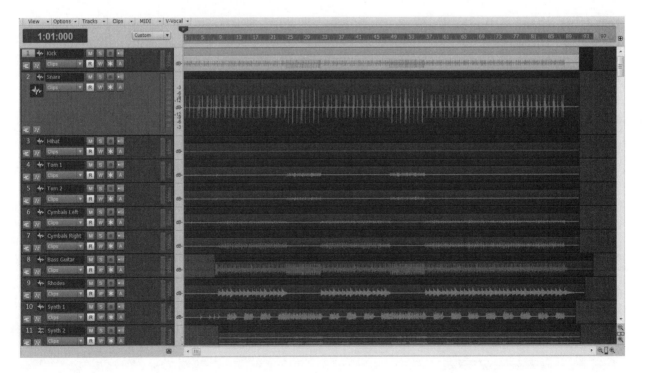

Figure 5.3. Track view

Tip: Track view has a redundant Time Display in the upper left-hand corner. This Time Display can be set to another scale. If you are doing video, you may want to set it to show frames. If you don't need a second time display, right-click the time display and select None from the menu. I usually hide it.

Figure 5.4. Hiding the Track view Time Display

Inspector Pane. Open and close the Inspector pane by using the keyboard shortcut I. The Inspector pane shows the Console view channel for the currently selected track. It will also show the corresponding bus channel if you expand the Inspector pane by grabbing the right edge. Click tabs along the top of the Inspector pane to show track properties, clip properties, and the ProChannel setup for the currently selected track. It normally docks to the left side of SONAR, but can also be moved to the right or detached to a separate floating window. The Inspector pane improves workflow by reducing the need to switch back and forth between Track view and Console view.

Browser. The Browser gives us access to media and files you might want to drag into your projects, such as loops, templates, and track colors. There are three tabs: the media tab for access to files; the plug-in tab for access to effects, and the synth tab for access to the Synth Rack. Open and close the browser with the keyboard shortcut B.

Figure 5.5. The Inspector pane

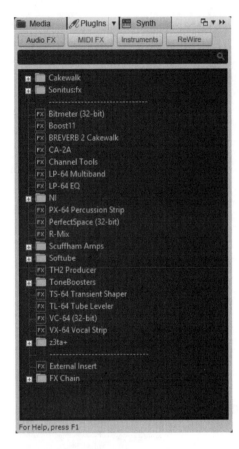

Figure 5.6. The Browser pane

MultiDock. Usually found at the bottom of the SONAR window, the MultiDock is a container for any of the other views you might want to open when working in SONAR. The two most essential views are the Console view and the Piano Roll view (PRV). If you have more than one view open at once, you can switch between them by using the tabs along the bottom. Open and close the MultiDock by using keyboard shortcut D. You can also view the MultiDock in full view by using Shift + D.

Figure 5.7. The MultiDock

Tip: To streamline SONAR, think of the Track view as your main workspace and keep the three additional panes closed until needed. Learn these three one-key shortcuts: I to open/close the Inspector, D to open/close the MultiDock, and B to open/close the Browser.

You can detach and float the entire MultiDock or any of the separate views. This is a huge advantage if you have a second monitor on your system. I usually keep Console view expanded to full screen on my second monitor, while leaving Track view on full screen on my primary monitor when working in my studio. When working remotely on my laptop, I size the MultiDock to cover Track view and switch back forth between Track view and the MultiDock by simply pressing D.

If the MultiDock is detached, right-click the upper left-hand corner and select Dock to return to the MultiDock area. Here you can scroll down through the various parameters.

Navigator pane. The Navigator pane represents a high-level overview of all the tracks over the full length of a project. It always reminds me of the overview in the 1980s arcade game Defender! Open it by using View > Navigator Show/Hide from the Track view menu. Size or move the view box to quickly focus on any area of a project. Normally, I leave the Navigator closed unless my project has lots of tracks.

Figure 5.8. Navigator pane

SONAR Projects

This section covers the essentials for creating, saving, and working with projects. This should help you get hands-on with SONAR

Creating a Project

By default, the Quick Start dialog box will show up every time you start SONAR. The Quick Start gives you direct access to Open Project, Open Recent Projects, Create a New Project, and Help. You can also do all of this under File in the SONAR Menu, similar to most Windows programs.

If you don't want the Quick Start dialog box to show up every time you start SONAR, uncheck the checkbox at the bottom labeled "Show This at Startup." Open the Quick Start dialog box at any time from the menu, under Help > Quick Start.

When you create a project, first enter the title and select where you want to save the file. By default, all of the files are stored inside a folder named with the project title. There is also an option to "Store Project Audio in Its Own Folder," which I highly recommend you keep that checked as an option. It makes backing up and moving your projects much more straightforward as all the media stays together.

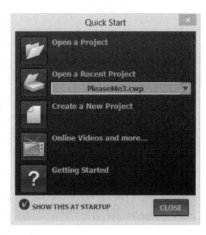

Figure 5.9. Quick Start dialog box

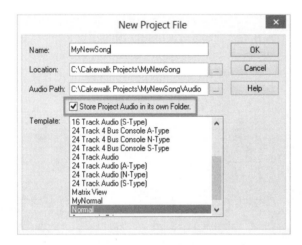

Figure 5.10. New Project file dialog box

Saving Your Project

When working in SONAR, press Ctrl + S to save. It is a great idea to save frequently and get in the habit of hitting Ctrl + S after any major edit or recording. SONAR projects are stored on your system, using the .cwp file extension.

If you use Save As from the File menu, you can save projects as a Template or as a Cakewalk Bundle. Templates serve as a starting point for new projects and have the file extension .cwt. When you create a new project, you can select from available Templates for a predefined configuration of tracks, effects, and Soft Synths. Cakewalk Bundles packs all project media into a single .bun file you can use to back up to other drives. Cakewalk Bundles is the main format used when sending a project file to another SONAR user online.

Figure 5.11. Save As file formats

Auto Save

To help protect against losing work, you can configure SONAR to automatically save periodically. Auto Save options are located in the Advanced section of the Preferences dialog box (P). If you have crash or power failure, SONAR will ask whether you want to restore from a backup.

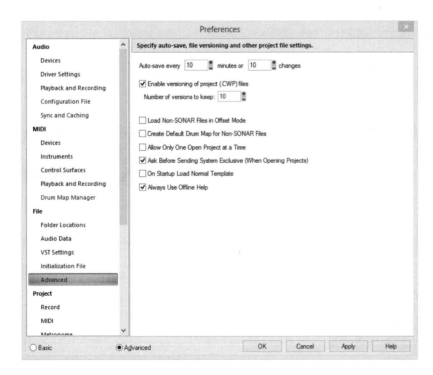

Figure 5.12. Auto Save options in preferences

Play, Stop, Rewind

SONAR has comprehensive options for navigating a project, but I want to introduce you to just some of the essentials. To give these a try, load one of the sample projects so you have something to play back.

To start playback, press the space bar. To stop playback, press the space bar again. During playback, a vertical line appears in the Track pane that shows the position of the Now Time. The SONAR manual doesn't have a specific name for the vertical line, but I simply call it the cursor.

By default, the cursor will return to the start position when you stop playback. If you don't like this (and I typically don't!), uncheck "On Stop, Rewind to Now Marker" to make the cursor park where you stop it. You can find this setting in the Track view menu under Options (Figure 5.13).

Figure 5.13. On Stop, rewind to Now Marker setting

To rewind to the beginning of the project, use the keyboard shortcut W, which is the return-to-zero (RTZ) shortcut. Note: SONAR supports a loop feature that allows loop playback over a defined section of the project. If looping is enabled when you press W, the cursor will return to the loop start. If you press W again, it will rewind to the beginning of the project.

To position the cursor and set the Now Time, click anywhere along the numbered part of time ruler, or grab the cursor pointer and drag it to the left or right. You can also position the cursor by clicking on clips or the background anytime the mouse pointer appears as an I-beam tool.

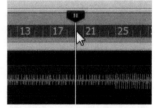

Figure 5.14. Positioning the cursor

The Control Bar transport module has a full set of transport controls, including a slider to quickly position the cursor to any part of the project. The controls behave like familiar controls from a tape transport—familiar, anyway, if you are old enough to have used tape machines!

Figure 5.15. The Transport module

Zooming In and Out

SONAR X2 features enhanced zooming over any previous version. If you move the mouse pointer to the top edge of the timeline, you will see a zoom magnifier pointer. Using this, you can drag up and down to zoom in and out horizontally.

Here are the essentials for zooming in SONAR:

Zoom horizontally. Left-click and drag up and down from the top edge of the time ruler. Note that the pointer changes to a special Zoom icon. As you zoom, you can also pan left and right by holding down the left mouse button. From the keyboard, zoom in and out horizontally by using Ctrl + Left Arrow and Ctrl + Right Arrow.

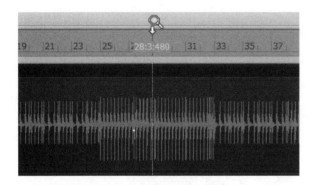

Figure 5.16. Timeline zooming

Zoom vertically. To zoom track heights vertically, right-click the time ruler and drag it up and down from the top edge. You can also resize the track height by dragging the lower edge of the track header in the Track pane. Another way to do this is with Ctrl + Up Arrow and Ctrl + Down Arrow.

Auto Track Zoom. SONAR also includes Auto Track Zoom for track height. This feature is turned off by default, but can be turned on under View > Auto Track Zoom in the Track view. Select any track and adjust the height. Now whenever you select another track, it will zoom to the same vertical height automatically. It is a great way to focus on your work without spending effort constantly resizing tracks.

Fast Zoom. Hold Alt and roll the mouse wheel to zoom in and out horizontally. Hold Alt + Shift and roll to zoom vertically. Several additional options for Fast Zoom are available on the Track view menu under Options > Mouse Wheel Zoom Options. In my experience, this does not work with all brands of mice, so you may need to test this with your system.

Zoom tool. Another way to zoom is to hold down Z to pull up the zoom tool and drag a selection around the area you want to magnify. Alt + Z will return to the previous zoom level.

Notice that the lower right corner of Track view contains dedicated controls for horizontal and vertical zoom if you want yet more ways to zoom in and out!

Figure 5.17. Track view zoom controls

Tip: You can access a couple of other really useful zooms from the Track view menu. View > Fit Tracks and Buses to Window and View > Fit Project to Window (Shift + F) both fit all the tracks in your project to the screen. You can also double-click the top half of the time ruler as another shortcut to Fit Project to Window.

Getting Help

Get context sensitive help for most SONAR features by pressing F1. You can find the full manual in the Windows Start Menu under Programs > Cakewalk > SONAR X2 Producer > SONAR X2 Producer Help(x64).

Use the code in Fig. 5.18 to access Cakewalk's online help resources, or use the code in Fig. 5.19 to download a PDF file of the SONAR X2 Reference Guide.

Figure 5.18. Cakewalk documentation QR Code

Figure 5.19. SONAR X2 reference guide QR Code

SONAR links you to the online help system to provide the most update information. If you don't have your SONAR computer connected to the Internet, or if you just prefer to use help from your hard drive, change the setting under Edit > Preferences > Advanced to "Always using offline help setting."

Tooltips show features' names and keyboard shortcuts when you hover the mouse over on-screen features. Tooltips is an excellent tool while learning SONAR, and I always leave them turned on. If for some reason you don't see Tooltips, turn them on under Edit > Preferences > Display > "Show Tooltips."

Chapter 6

THE CONTROL BAR

The Control Bar contains transport controls, counters, and direct access buttons to all kinds of SONAR features. In this chapter, you will learn how to configure the Control Bar and how to use the four most essential modules.

> **Tip:** If you accidentally lose the Control Bar, bring it back by pressing C or navigate in the menu to Views > Control Bar. If you don't want the Control Bar hidden, consider assigning the shortcut C to some other function to avoid misplacing the Control Bar!

Figure 6.1. The SONAR Control Bar

Configuring the Control Bar

Configure the Control Bar by right-clicking anywhere on it, excluding buttons. This reveals the Control Bar options menu (Figure 6.2), with options to detach it or dock it at the bottom. I think it works best to just leave it docked at the top of the screen.

Use the right-click options to hide or show the Control Bar modules. I prefer to keep the Control Bar simple. I strongly suggest, if you are just starting with SONAR, to keep only the following modules: Tools, Snap, Transport, and Loop. This gives you ready access to the essential tools, while keeping the Control Bar clean and simple.

You can reorder modules by grabbing the left edge and dragging it within the Control Bar. The default order works fine for the first four modules.

Figure 6.2. Control Bar options

Tools Module

The Tools module has quick access buttons to the editing tools in SONAR. The tool farthest left on the module is the Smart tool. Ninety-five percent of operations within SONAR X2 can be done by using the Smart tool, including selecting, moving, and modifying clips and events. Make sure the Smart tool icon is selected; if it's not, click the Smart tool or use keyboard shortcut F5.

Figure 6.3. The Control Bar Tools module

Other tools can be selected by using Tools module buttons or corresponding keyboard shortcuts. Starting with F5, the shortcuts go up the keyboard sequentially:

- Smart tool (F5)
- Select tool (F6)
- Move tool (F7)
- Edit tool (F8)
- Draw tool (F9)
- Erase tool (F10)

Note: The Edit tool has an arrow on the lower right corner. Many buttons on the Control Bar have an arrow like this. The arrow indicates additional right-click options. In this case, you can choose what should appear on this button—the Edit tool, the Timing tool, or the Split tool.

Figure 6.4. Draw tool and Event Draw duration buttons

Below the six selecting tools button is another button called Event Draw Duration. It is associated with the Draw tool and is highlighted whenever the Draw tool is selected. Right-clicking the button allows you to set a musical value, such as eighth notes. This sets the length of MIDI notes when drawing them in Piano Roll view with Snap turned on.

Snap Module

The Snap module has buttons and settings that establishes the timing grid and aligns clips and notes when editing. When the top left button (the one with the 3 x 3 grid) is illuminated, the snap feature is active. Keyboard shortcut N also turns Snap on and off.

The Snap right-click menu also has option for other Snap modes. With Snap turned on, as you moved clips within the Track view, you'll see they snap based on the increments set up in the grid settings.

If you set a quarter-note grid, dragging and dropping a clip will automatically line it up to the nearest beat. Likewise, if you set the grid to eighth notes, clips will line up to the nearest eighth.

SONAR X2 debuts a new Smart Grid mode that sets the snap grid based on how far you zoom in. If you zoom way out, snapping occurs by full bars. However, as you zoom in more, you get smaller and smaller snap increments. This can be a very efficient way to work once you get used to it.

Next to the Grid setting button are two useful modifier buttons. The button labeled "3" sets the grid to triplet values. The button to the right of "3" enables snapping to dotted values.

Figure 6.5. The Control Bar Snap module

The Snap to Landmark Events button resembles a mountain with a flag. Clicking this button turns Landmark snapping on and off. Right-click to choose additional options to snap to, including markers, clips, automation nodes, and Now Time.

Transport Module

The Transport module has obvious controls, such as Play, Stop, Pause, and Record. Play and Pause can also be toggled by using the space bar. Like any system emulating a tape recorder, there are also Rewind and Fast Forward buttons. To the left of the slider, below the main buttons, is Return to Zero (RTZ), which can also be accessed by using keyboard shortcut W. Drag the slider anywhere within the song or just click on a specific point to jump to a particular position. This gives you a general, relative position with the song. The slider moves as the song plays. The button to the right of the slider will allow you to jump to the end of the song.

Figure 6.6. The Control Bar Transport module

Use the Record button (R) to start recording in SONAR on any tracks armed for recording. Notice that the Record button has a little arrow in the lower right corner. The arrow indicates there are additional right-click options, which in this case is a shortcut to the Record page within the Preferences dialog box. There you can find a variety of setup options for recording, which we will review in detail in a later chapter.

The Time Display section of the Transport modules shows Now Time in big numbers, along with other project properties. The Now Time is the exact time position either currently playing or that will play if you start playback. The Now Time is indicated by vertical cursor line. You can change the format of the time ruler by right-clicking on it (Figure 6.7). I set this option to include measures, beats, and ticks when doing music production.

Figure 6.7. Time Ruler Display
options

In the lower left of the Time Display are icons for the audio and MIDI engines. These are for troubleshooting if you are having playback problems or are using external MIDI synthesizers when a note gets stuck. The Time Display also shows the project's current sample rate and bit depth.

If you want to change the project tempo, double-click on the tempo shown in the Time Display and edit the value. In the lower right-hand corner, you will see the current time signature. Double-click it to open the Meter/Key Signature dialog box. This works fine for fixed tempo songs, but for full control over tempo and meter, you will want to work with the Tempo view (Views > Tempo).

A column of three buttons to the right of the Transport module controls the metronome click. The top one turns on the metronome for playback or during playback. The middle one turns on the metronome, while you're recording. The bottom one opens the metronome settings in the Preferences dialog box.

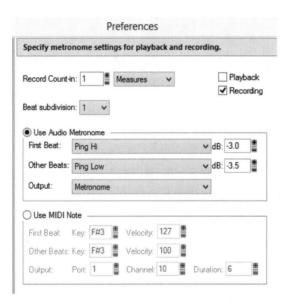

Figure 6.8. Metronome options

Loop Module

Click the top button in the Loop module to toggle looping on and off. You can also use the keyboard shortcut L to toggle looping. With looping on, the section of your song defined by the loop start and end times are repeated over and over. This is useful for focusing on EQ tweaks, creating beats, or loop recording.

The Set Loop Points to Selection button (Shift + L) is key to setting up a loop. You can also set a loop by dragging a selection on the time ruler or within the project and the button.

Figure 6.9. The Control
Bar Loop module

When Loop is on, start and end markers appear on the time ruler, connected by a yellow bar. You can adjust the loop times by dragging them from either end. You can also drag the entire Loop forward and backward in time.

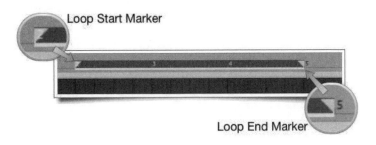

Figure 6.10. Loop start and end markers

This part of the module shows you the Loop in and out points at any given time. It's great to have this module open so you can easily turn Loop on and off. Looping is extremely helpful when you're auditioning for mixing or also for Loop recording.

That's an introduction to the Control Bar the most essential modules. We will use these tools and some of the other modules as we continue to explore recording and editing in SONAR.

Chapter 7
TRACKS AND CLIPS

I introduced Track view and the concept of clips in an earlier chapter. In this chapter, I will detail how to use tracks and clips and the functions of their controls.

The main SONAR workspace, Track view, is made up of the Track pane on the left and the Clips pane on the right. The actual tracks are rows that contain the audio recordings or instrument (MIDI) data. The recording is represented along a horizontal timeline with the time ruler at the top. The recording may be a sound (e.g., a lead vocal) or it may be a MIDI (e.g., the notes of a synth line). The Track view organization is roughly analogous to a multitask tape machine, but is far more visual and flexible.

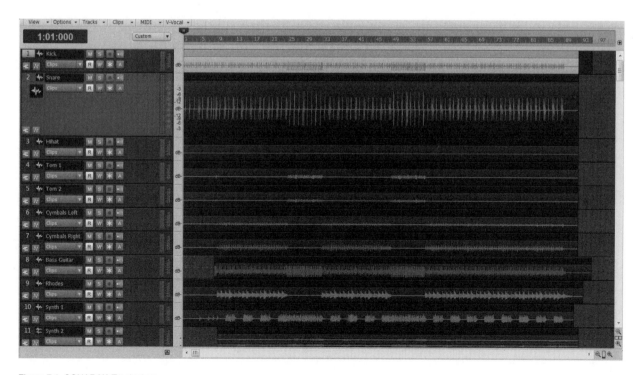

Figure 7.1. SONAR X2 Track view

Working with Tracks

You can always find Track view under View > Track view (Alt + 1), if it happens to be hidden. Note that Track view has its own set of menus at the top that gives you convenient access to a nice selection of view options and editing tools.

Rearranging Tracks

Rearrange tracks by grabbing the track strip and dragging it up or down the Track pane. As you drag, a red bar will appear that shows where it will be placed when you drop it. Note: Drag from the blank area directly below the track number, as shown in Fig. 7.2.

Figure 7.2. Dragging to rearrange tracks

Adding Tracks

Right-click on any empty space within the Track pane or any of the Track strips to show a context menu. I often refer to this as the right-click menu. Use the right-click menu to insert an audio track, a MIDI track, multiple tracks, a track folder, or a track from a template. Inserting a track from a template allows you to have a preconfigured setup to include plug-in effects and instruments. Instrument tracks are better added from the Browser, which I will go over in a later chapter.

Figure 7.3. Adding a track, using the right-click menu

Deleting Tracks

To delete a track, select its track number, right-click, and select Delete Track. To delete several tracks at once at once, select several tracks and complete the same steps. You can also delete selected tracks from the Track view menu under Track > Delete Track (Figure 7.4). Note that the menu adapts to the number of tracks you have selected.

Figure 7.4. Deleting tracks from the Track view menu

Cloning Tracks

Cloning is what SONAR calls copying as it relates to tracks. To clone, highlight the track number, then right-click and select Clone Track. This pops up the Clone Track(s) dialog box (Figure 7.5), which offers several options of what to include in the newly cloned track. The most important thing is to decide if you want to clone Events. In this context, Events are any audio or MIDI clips that you may have already recorded.

Figure 7.5. The Clone Track(s) dialog box

Tip: I like to use Clone Track to create a new blank track that has the same setup as a track I have already been working with. To do this, just deselect Clone Events as you clone the track.

Track Strip Features

Each track strip has a set of controls called widgets. There are several presets to configure which widgets you want shown under the Track Control menu (Figure 7.6). Use the Track Control Manager to customize which widgets are shown for each preset. Let's go over the most common of the track strip widgets:

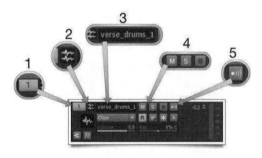

Figure 7.6. Track strip widgets: Part 1

1. **Track Number.** The track number is automatically set based on the current position. Click the number to select a track. The track number for a selected track appears with a blue-highlighted background. To select several tracks, swipe across the track numbers of several tracks while holding down the left mouse button.

2. **Track Type Icon.** This icon indicates the type of track. A little wave shape is shown for an audio track; and a little keyboard shape, for an instrument track. If you're on an instrument track, double-clicking the icon will bring up the window for the associated Soft Synth.

3. **Track Name.** Double-click the track name to edit the name. F2 will also open the track name for editing—just as in most Windows programs.

4. **Mute, Solo, Record.** The Mute button silences the track, the Solo Button silences all other tracks, and the Record button arms the track for recording. To record audio or MIDI to a track, you need to first arm that particular track for recording, by using the track strip Record button, then press Record on the Control Bar (keyboard shortcut R).

5. **Input Echo.** Enable Input Echo to pass audio from the hardware input to the output as configured for the track. This allows you to hear through that track while recording. This is essential when using virtual instruments or guitar amp simulators. For normal audio recordings, such as recording a singer, you might want to monitor the voice in a more direct way. Input Echo will have some latency, based on your audio interface driver setting. I will go into more detail later on when we explore recording.

6. **Minimize Track Strip.** This button is a quick way to minimize the track strip. It works as a toggle to minimize or restore the track height.

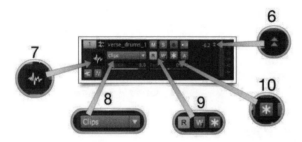

Figure 7.7. Track strip widgets: Part 2

7. **Track Icon.** To change one of these icons, simply right-click and select "Load Track Icon." You'll see that it comes up with set of folders allowing you to choose a different icon file. SONAR has a wide range of clip art instruments from which to choose. I usually use solid colors for the icons and set all similar tracks to the same color. You can also set the track icon by dragging in images from the Media tab of the Browser.

8. **Edit Filter.** The Edit Filter selection allows you to choose an automation envelope to overlay on the Clips pane. Most of the time, you will want this set to "Clips." Prior to the SONAR X2 release, the Edit Filter was the only way to work with automation envelopes. Now, Automation lanes are a better solution. You will use the Edit Filter to show Audio Transients for AudioSnap and for quick access to clip gain.

9. **Automate Read/Write.** When the R button is highlighted, the track is in Automation Read mode. When the W button is highlighted, the track is ready to write automation. Automation is a powerful feature for adding a dynamic element to your mixes. Use automation to remember changes to volume you make in real time during playback. You can use automation for just about any parameter that has a knob, slider, or button in SONAR.

10. **Track Freeze.** When you have a big project with a lot of effects and virtual instruments, it might get difficult for the computer to handle all the work during playback. The result can be dropouts or glitches. That's where the Freeze button comes into play. Click the Freeze button to quickly rerecord or "freeze" a track. Track Freeze renders a new audio file that takes all the CPU-hogging instruments and

effects offline. Click again to unfreeze. I also use Track Freeze after comping a part from takes. More on this later in the book.

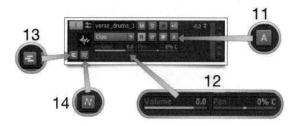

Figure 7.8. Track strip widgets: Part 3

11. **Archive.** The Archive button takes a track completely offline. The track will not play or use any CPU power. Clicking again puts the track back online. Note that you cannot change the Archive state during playback. This is a great option when you aren't sure if you need the track but don't want to delete it or keep it muted.
12. **Volume & Pan.** Use these widgets for quick access to track volume and panning. It is often more convenient to use the larger controls in the Inspector pane or the Console view, but they are convenient for quick adjustments during recording.
13. **Take Lanes Open/Close.** SONAR X2 allows you to record multiple takes to a single track. If you have done this, click this button to show all the takes. You can select your favorite take or build a composite using the best parts.
14. **Automation Lanes Open/Close.** Before the X2 version, we could only use Edit Filter to see automation envelopes one at a time. Now when you click this button, you can see all the automation parameters as parallel lanes, which is a huge improvement.

Track Control Manager

In the previous section, I identified the most common track strip widgets. Even more are available. You can customize the track strip by using the Track Control Manager from the track strip menu. Here you can select exactly which widgets you would like to see for each type of track. I like the track strip to be as simple as possible and use the Inspector pane to control the details.

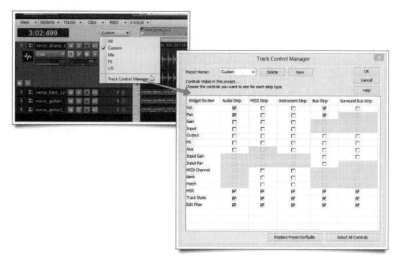

Figure 7.9. The Track Control Manager

Time Ruler

The Time Ruler lives along the top of the Clips pane. By default, the time divisions are set to M:B:T (measures, beats, ticks). This works great for many kinds of music production. Click anywhere along the ruler to set the Now Time and position the cursor. If you have Snap to Grid turned on, the Now Time will snap to the nearest grid division. You can also position the Now Time by clicking anywhere on the background or clicking on the top part of any clip by using the Smart tool. To change the time format of the Time Ruler, right-click on it and select from other popular formats. If I am working with a freely played live recording, I change this to H:M:S:F (hours, minutes, seconds, frames).

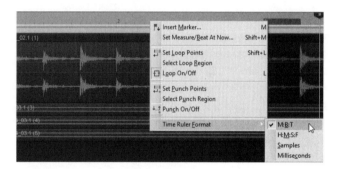

Figure 7.10. Changing the Time Ruler format

Looping Playback

Use the Time Ruler along with the Loop module in the Control Bar to set up looped playback. Here are the steps:

1. Drag across the Time Ruler to draw in where you want to loop.

Figure 7.11. Selecting where to loop

2. Set the loop markers by using the Control Bar or Shift + L.

Figure 7.12. Set the loop markers

3. Now you can turn the loop on or off by using the Loop button or keyboard shortcut L.

Figure 7.13. Turning the
loop on or off

When the cursor reaches the loop end marker, it will jump to the loop start marker and continue to repeat the loop until you stop playback or turn Loop off. You can drag the loop markers to a new position or drag the markers from either end to move the loop start point and the loop end point.

Figure 7.14. Adjusting the loop end marker

Adding Markers to the Time Ruler

Position the cursor in the Time Ruler and press M. This opens the Marker dialog box. Type in a name for the marker and click OK.

Figure 7.15. Adding a marker to the Time Ruler

Markers are particularly helpful for identifying song sections in your project. You can move them by dragging the flag. Markers become even more useful if you display the Markers module in the Control bar. The Markers module has a drop-down list to instantly jump to any marker in the project. It also has buttons to add a marker, jump to the next, and jump to the previous marker.

Figure 7.16. Moving a marker

If you are working on a long project with lots of markers, Open the dedicated Marker view (Views > Markers) in the MultiDock. Here you can navigate by markers, delete, and rename them.

Track Folders

SONAR allows you group tracks into track folders. To do this, select some tracks by swiping over the track numbers, then right-click and choose Move to Folder. From here, choose an existing track folder or create a new one.

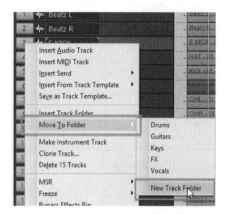

Figure 7.17. Right-click to create a track folder

This works great for organizing drum tracks or background vocals. All the related tracks are indented under the folder and can be muted or soloed from the controls on the track strip for the folder.

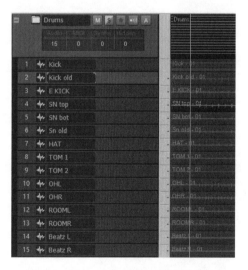

Figure 7.18. Drums organized into a track folder

Click the +/– icon at the left side of the track folder to open or close it. This is a great way to maintain control of large projects!

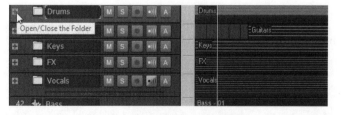

Figure 7.19. Closed track folders

Bus Pane

Track view has a special pane called the Bus pane. Open and close it with the Show/ Hide Bus Pane button at the bottom of the Track pane, or use keyboard shortcut Shift + B. This allows you to click on the buses and access all the features from the Inspector without needing to switch to Track view.

Buses serve as points for submixes and for adding common effects when mixing. All projects have at least one bus channel—the Master. All other channels are mixed to the Master bus, at which point you would commonly apply effects. We will cover the details of buses later on.

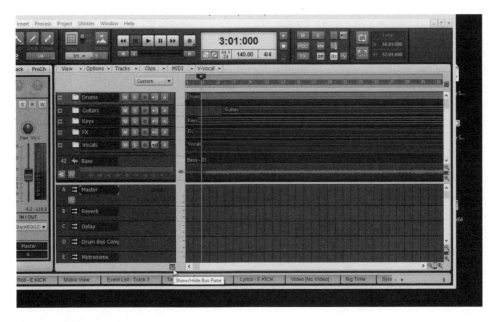

Figure 7.20. Open and close the Bus pane

I've covered all the basics of the tracks and clips. Now let's take a closer look at the Inspector.

Chapter 8
THE INSPECTOR

The Inspector pane shows a mixer channel for a selected track. We introduced this earlier as a key component of the Skylight UI. Because the Inspector shows a sliver of the Console view mixer, you don't need to flip back and forth between Track view and Console view while working in SONAR.

Working with the Inspector Pane

In addition to the mixer channel, the Inspector pane can show a track's associated bus channel, the ProChannel, track properties, and clip properties. But before we go any further, let's review the basics of working with the Inspector pane.

Opening the Inspector Pane. Open and close the Inspector pane by using keyboard shortcut I. You can also open it from the main menu (View > Inspector). The Inspector pane is usually docked on the left side of the SONAR, but can be floated, or docked, to the right side. I prefer it on the left. If your Inspector is floating, drop it near the left edge of SONAR to dock it.

Showing the Bus Channel. Every channel in SONAR routes to either a submix bus (if you set one up) or the Master bus. One excellent feature of the Inspector is its ability to show the bus associated with the selected channel. If you don't see it, grab the right edge of the Inspector pane and resize it to reveal the bus channel. You can also hide or narrow the view of the bus channel by dragging the right edge.

Displaying MIDI Properties. If you are working with a MIDI track or Instrument track, click the MIDI tab at the bottom of the bus channel to see the MIDI properties. In this mode, the Sends section changes to Bank and Patch info. The bus channel is replaced with the following MIDI properties: Chorus/Reverb, Snap to Scale, Input Quantize, Arpeggiator, Key, and Time Offsets.

Figure 8.1. The SONAR Inspector pane

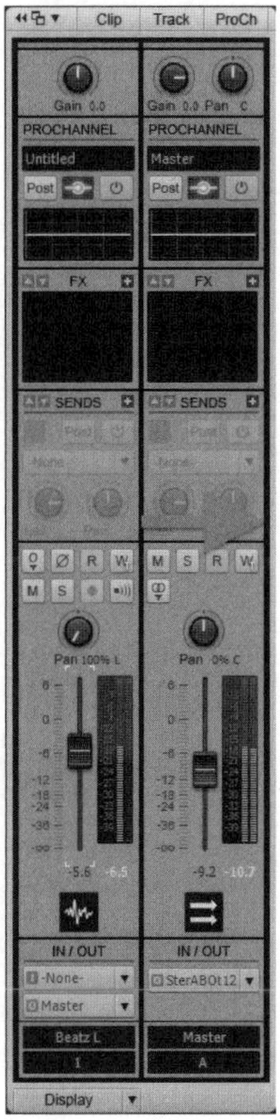

Figure 8.2. Showing the associated bus channel

Figure 8.3. Inspector pane
MIDI properties

Opening the ProChannel. Click the tab labeled "ProCh" at the top of the Inspector to access the selected channel's entire ProChannel setup. This is a huge time saver as it negates the need to switch back to Console view, find the correct channel, open the ProChannel, and change the settings.

Figure 8.4. Showing the ProChannel in the Inspector pane

Showing Clip Properties. Click the tab labeled "Clip" at the top of the Inspector to show detailed properties for the selected clip. Here you see and edit detailed properties, including the clip name, colors, and Groove clip options.

Figure 8.5. Clip properties

Showing Track Properties. Click the "Track" tab to show the track properties at the top of the Inspector. It gives you a consolidated view of all track properties, including the track name, AudioSnap setup, Automation modes, colors, and a space to write notes.

Figure 8.6. Track properties

Channel Display Options

As with so many aspects of SONAR, you can choose which features show up on the mixer channel in the Inspector. A similar setup in Console view allows you to configure the Console view mixer channels differently.

Click on the arrow next to Display at the bottom of the Inspector pane. Check or uncheck the various options to turn on or off sections of the channel. Occasionally, I turn off Input Gain or the Icon to save some screen space. For the most part, however, I leave all of them on.

Figure 8.7. Inspector Display options menu

Mixer Channel Details

The mixer channel in the Inspector pane is exactly the same as the channel in the Console view. Let's go over the controls available on each channel:

1. **Input Gain.** Input Gain allows you boost or cut the level coming into the channel. This occasionally comes in handy, though I tend to use clip gain automation instead. If you don't use Input Gain, you can turn it off in the Inspector Display options, as described in the previous paragraph.

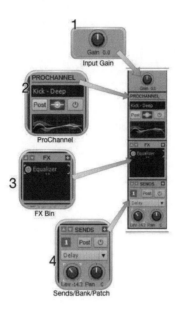

Figure 8.8. Console channel controls—top half

2. **ProChannel.** This section contains controls for the ProChannel, as well as for the small EQ Graph for the ProChannel EQ. The controls here include the ProChannel preset management, the Post button to route the ProChannel after the FX Bin, the signal indicator, the ProChannel On/Off button, and the EQ Graph.

3. **FX Bin.** The FX Bin section is used to control effects inserted on that channel. It includes a button to bypass it entirely to take the effects offline. To add and new effect, click the plus sign (+) and select an effect plug-in. You can also drag effects from the Browser to the FX Bin.

4. **Sends/Bank/Patch.** For audio channels, this part of the channel shows FX Sends to effects (FX) buses. Here, you will find the Send Level knob and Pan knob. You can also set the Send post fader or turn it off entirely. For MIDI channels, you can switch it to show the synth Bank and Patch management details.

5. **MSR.** The MSR section has many buttons and controls, including those for mute, solo, and record; for automation read and write; for input echo; and for mono/stereo and phase invert. There are so many buttons, however, that I need a separate figure (Figure 8.9) to indicate what all the buttons are for.

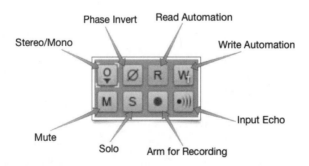

Figure 8.9. The MSR section buttons

6. **Pan Knob.** The Pan knob works as you expect, by positioning a signal in the stereo spectrum between the left or right speakers. Note: The Pan knob works as a balance control on stereo tracks. For example, as you turn the knob to the right, the left channel is turned down.

Tip: For separate left and right panning control for stereo tracks, try using the Channel Tools plug-in instead.

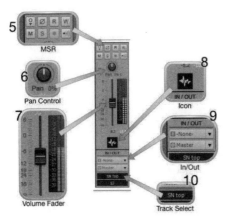

Figure 8.10. Console channel controls—bottom half

7. **Volume Fader.** The Volume fader and meter are the key mixing tools on a channel. Drag the fader up and down, or use your mouse wheel. For finer control, hold down the Shift key as you move the fader. Double-click the Volume fader to set it to 0 dB. If you right-click the meter, you can choose how the meters work. By default, the metering is set to Peak, but I advise setting these to show Peak + RMS. The RMS is an average of the level and a better representation of apparent loudness.

Figure 8.11. Channel Meter Display options

8. **Icon.** Use the Icon to identify the type of track by assigning a picture. Select from a variety of clip art images by right-clicking the Icon or by dragging images from the Browser. I prefer to use the solid-color Icons; however, pictures of guitars, drum kits, and most every other kind of instrument are available.

9. **In/Out.** Use the top drop-down list to select from the available inputs on your audio interface. This determines where the signal will come from when recording to the associated track. Use the lower drop-down list to select the bus you want the channel to route to. By default, this will be the Master bus for new channels, but you can assign it to other buses, hardware outputs, or FX side chains.

10. **Track Name.** Just above the track number at the bottom is the track name. Click it to open a list of all the available tracks and buses. If you select a different track, the Inspector will switch to show the corresponding channel.

Chapter **9**

THE BROWSER

The SONAR Browser pane gives you access to loops, Soft Synths, and effects. Open and close the Browser with the keyboard shortcut B. Normally, the Browser opens along the right side, but it can be detached, moved to the left side, or docked as a tab in the MultiDock.

The Browser also offers the ability to search for media files and plug-ins. You can drag most types of media files (e.g., drum loops) from the Browser and drop them onto tracks in your project. This is a fun and efficient way to work.

Media Browser

Click the tab labeled "Media" to switch to the Media Browser (Figure 9.1). The Media Browser is similar in concept to Windows File Explorer. By default, the Media Browser shows a simple view of the files on your system. Click on the Location Presets menu to browse, starting at predefined folders. When you select one (e.g., the Audio Library), you will see that location's files and folders in the File List. Navigate through the File List by double-clicking folders to open them or by clicking the Up One Level button to go back.

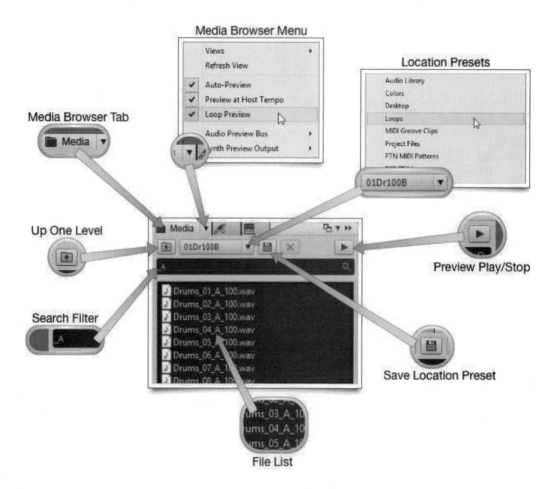

Figure 9.1. Media Browser

For increased browsing control, enable the Views > Folders option in the Browser menu. This will open a full tree view of your file system in a Folders pane to left.

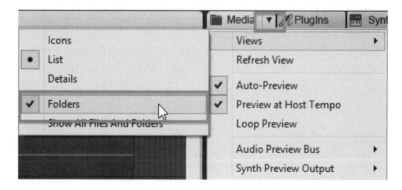

Figure 9.2. Showing folders in the Media Browser

Keep in mind that you can detach the Browser or move it to the MultiDock. This will cause the files to appear on the right as you navigate through the folder on the left.

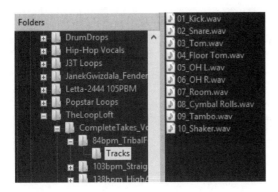

Figure 9.3. Media Browser with folders

The folder pane allows you to jump to the Windows File Explorer from the right-click menu. Just right-click the any folder and select Open. This cannot be done from the simpler File List.

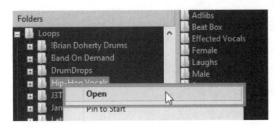

Figure 9.4. Opening a file in Windows File Explorer

Previewing Loops

Navigate to any audio or MIDI file on your system and click to hear a preview at the project tempo. Stop the preview by clicking the preview Play/Stop button. Note: If you don't hear playback, make sure the audio preview bus is selected in the Media Browser menu. The menu also allows you to turn off Auto Preview and Preview at Host Tempo.

Figure 9.5. Media Browser Preview options

The Loop Preview option will do exactly that—loop the playback of the selected media file. This is particularly useful when auditioning drum loops and riffs against your project tracks. When you find something that works, drag it to a track or double-click to add it to the selected track at the Now Time.

Importing/Exporting

You can drag audio media files from the Browser and drop them in your project. If you drag a file to blank space in the Track pane, a new track is automatically created, along with a clip for the file. If you drag several at once, new tracks will be created for all of them. This is great when importing multitrack drums or importing all the tracks of a song recorded on another system.

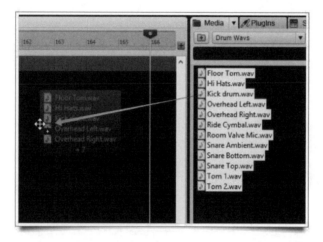

Figure 9.6. Importing by drag and drop

This works the other way around for exporting. Select one or more clips and drag them from Track view to the Browser to export as .wav or MIDI files. This is a quick way to create your own custom loop library!

Assigning Track Icons

The Location Presets list includes a location for track icons. Select this list, find the name of the icon, and drag it to a track to set the track icon. I prefer to use the color icons rather than clip art, so I set a new location preset to the color icons folder. Just navigate to the color icons and click the Save Location Preset button. Now I can set my track colors by dragging the color icons straight to the tracks!

> **Tip:** If you feel ambitious, you can create your own track icons. Use any editor and save the images as 96x96 .bmp files. Store them with the other icon files or create a Location Preset for your custom icons. The easiest way is to duplicate one of the existing color files, rename it, and edit it with Windows Paint. This is how I created LiteBlue.bmp that you see listed in Fig. 9.7.

Figure 9.7. Track colors in the Media
Browser

Using Track Templates

SONAR comes with a Location Preset that points to lots of factory track templates.
Drag any of these templates to the Track pane to create a track with a preset name,
insert FX, ProChannel setup, and track icon.

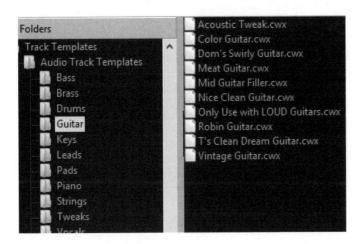

Figure 9.8. Track templates in the Media Browser

It is very interesting to load track template presets, to see how certain type of
tracks might be processed. To save your own track templates, right-click on any track
number and click Save as Track Template. You can save a track template for any type
of track, but the templates are particularly helpful for working with multioutput and
multitimbral Soft Synth setups, as you will learn later in the book.

Plug-in Browser

The Plug-in Browser is the best way to locate and apply effects and instruments to your
project. Drag effects from the Browser to a track or to the FX bin section in the Console

view or Inspector. You can also browse for Soft Synth plug-ins. Note. In SONAR, the word "effects" and the abbreviation "FX" are used interchangeably. The terms "Instrument," "Virtual Instrument," and "Soft Synth" are also used interchangeably.

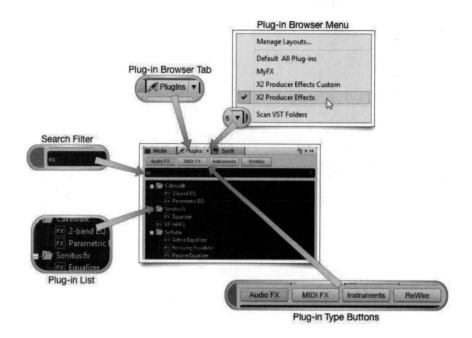

Figure 9.9. The Plug-in Browser

Browsing Plug-ins

Click on the Browser Plug-ins tab then select the type of plug-in: Audio FX, MIDI FX, Instruments, or ReWire. Drag the plug-in you want to a track, clip, or channel FX bin. I normally use the Browser when working with effects plug-ins but you can also work with MIDI FX, Instruments, and ReWire from this tab.

Searching Plug-ins

When you have dozens and dozens of plug-ins on your system, it can really speed things up to use the Search Filter. Just type in a few characters of the plug-in name to quickly filter through the plug-in list.

Manage Layouts

Open the Plug-in Browser menu to select from the available layouts. By default, you will see two options: "X2 Producer Effects" and "Default All Plug-ins." To create your own customized view of the effects, choose Manage Layouts. This opens the Cakewalk Plug-in Manager (also available via Utilities > Cakewalk Plug-in Manager). Use the tools here to create folders, organize, and rename the customized view of your plug-ins.

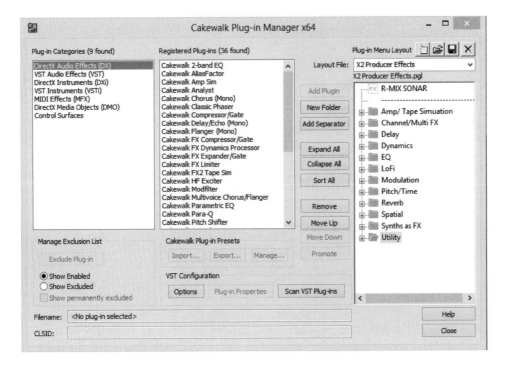

Figure 9.10. The Cakewalk Plug-in Manager

Synth Rack Browser

The Synth tab in the Browser is a consolidated view of all the Soft Synths running on your system. You can use the Synth Rack to manage, add, or delete Soft Synth instances.

In actual hardware, a sound module is essentially a rack of electronics you connect to a keyboard controller as a way to playback synthesized or sampled sounds. In SONAR, a Soft Synth is a virtualized sound module.

Tracks that work with Soft Synths are called Instrument tracks and MIDI tracks. The SONAR manual usually uses the wording "Soft Synths," "Synths," or "Software Instruments." The rest of the DAW industry refers to them as "Virtual Instruments." Keep in mind, however, that despite the name, all the terms refer to the same thing: a software-based sound module.

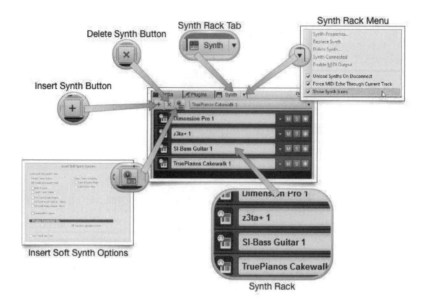

Figure 9.11. Synth Rack Browser

Inserting/Deleting Soft Synths

To insert a Soft Synth, click on the Insert Synth Button, choose Insert Synth, and select one from the list.

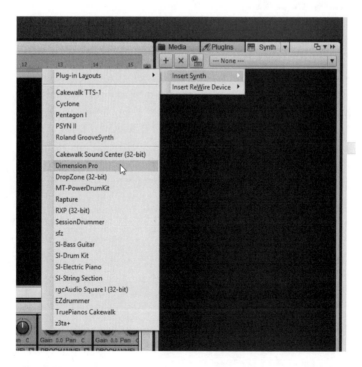

Figure 9.12. Insert Synth menu

By default, the Insert Soft Synth Options dialog will appear every time you do this. The most common option is to choose Simple instrument track, which sets up one instrument track with one Soft Synth. I will cover how to use the Insert Soft Synth Options to handle multioutput drum instruments later in the book.

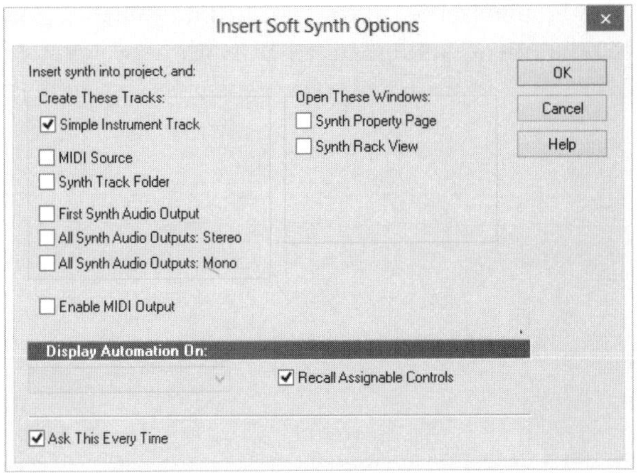

Figure 9.13. Soft Synth options

> **Tip:** If you always use Simple Instrument Tracks, clear the option Ask This Every Time at the bottom of the Insert Soft Synth Options dialog box. You can always access the Insert Soft Synth Options again with the dedicated button.

After you add the Soft Synth, it will appear in the Synth Rack list (the SONAR Manual calls this the Instrument list).

Synth Rack

The Synth Rack is a list of all Soft Synth instances you have currently loaded. Each Soft Synth has its own virtual rack, with controls for opening, deleting, and renaming. It also has direct controls for Soft Synth Mute, Solo, and Freeze.

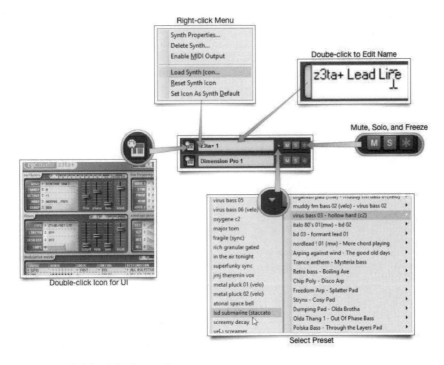

Figure 9.14. Soft Synth Rack controls

This should serve as a good introduction to the Browser and all its controls. You will understanding better how to take full advantage of the Browser as we explore recording and editing with SONAR.

PART II: RECORDING AND EDITING

Chapter 10
RECORDING AUDIO

When I was ten, I experimented with sound-on-sound recording by dubbing between two cassette decks. Both then and today, I find recording to be of the most enjoyable and fascinating things to do. With SONAR, you can record practically unlimited tracks with an astounding level of sound quality.

The focus of this chapter is recording audio. We'll start with the basics, before moving into recording takes, loop recording, and recording with a guitar amp simulator. I will also cover the best way to configure SONAR for an efficient recording workflow. Let's get started!

Hit Record

Here are the basic steps to recording audio in SONAR:

1. Connect a mic to one of the inputs on your audio interface. Test the mic and adjust the preamp gain to make sure there is a signal.

Figure 10.1. Connect your mic

2. Create an audio track in SONAR by right-clicking a blank area in the Track pane and selecting Insert Audio Track.

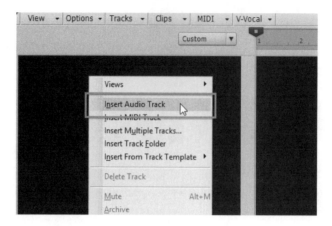

Figure 10.2. Inserting an audio track

3. Open the Inspector and match the track input to the same input to which your mic is connected.

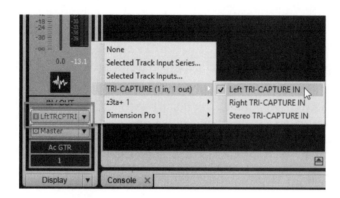

Figure 10.3. Set the input

4. Rename the track appropriately and arm it for recording by using the track strip Record button controls. Note: SONAR figures out if you want to record mono or stereo audio clips by looking at which type of input you select.

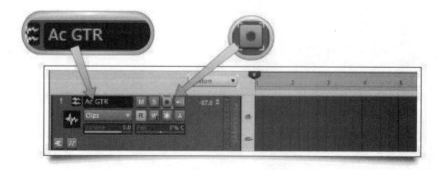

Figure 10.4. Arm for recording

4. Hit the Record button on the Control Bar or press R to start recording!

Figure 10.5. Hit Record!

5. Play something amazing, then hit the space bar to stop. Press W to rewind, then the space bar again to listen to what you've recorded. If it's great, be happy. If it sucks, then hit Ctrl + Z to undo, and return to step 1!

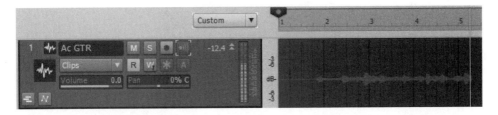

Figure 10.6. Recording in process

All SONAR recording follows those basic steps, but what about hearing yourself as you record? What about referencing a metronome click? What about overdubbing?

Setting up a Metronome Click

It is often helpful to hear a metronome click while recording. Enable the Metronome During Recording button in the Transport module to hear the click during recording. You can also use the Metronome During Playback button to choose whether to hear the click during playback.

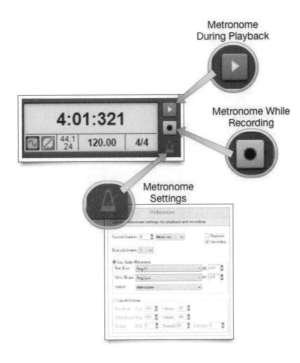

Figure 10.7. Using the SONAR Metronome

Click the Metronome Settings button to jump to the Metronome page in the Preferences dialog box. Here, you can choose the number of count-in measures, the Beat subdivision (number of clicks per measure), and the metronome sound. The Output setting selects the bus channel to which the metronome click is routed. Normally, there is a specific bus for the metronome, depending on the template used to create your project. Use the metronome bus to Level fader to control the volume of the click.

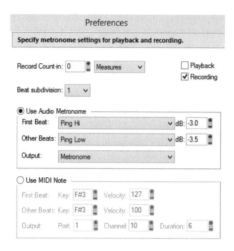

Figure 10.8. Metronome settings

Input Monitoring for Vocals

This section applies to recording with microphones—particularly vocals. When recording with a microphone, most artists use headphones to listen to themselves and any previously recorded tracks. I suggest using the built-in mixer in your audio interface, or your studio-mixing console. This mixes the mic directly to your headphones, along with the playback of existing tracks from SONAR. For this technique, make sure the Input Echo button is off on the track you are recording to, or else you will hear an annoying echo or feedback.

> **Tip:** Unless you have a studio with a separate control room, it is best to mute or turn off your studio monitors when tracking with a mic. The sound from the monitors will cause bleed-through to your track or will cause feedback when you open the mic.

Any audio passing through SONAR is subject to a delay in the range of 12 to 200 milliseconds as the computer calculates the mix. The amount of delay depends on the speed of your computer, the type of interface, and how you have the mixing latency parameters set. When latency is high (over 60 ms), you experience a delay between when you sing and when you hear it in your headphones. Below 60 ms, latency can result in an annoying phasing of your voice or while singing. Above 60 ms, it might even sound like noticeable echo. In either event, it can throw off your performance and timing.

All modern audio interfaces have a way to handle low-latency and zero-latency monitoring. There are often dedicated mix buttons or knobs on the audio interface itself, like on the Roland Tri-Capture (Figure 10.9); or on the DSP mixer app, like on the Roland Octa-Capture or PreSonus AudioBox (Figure 10.10).

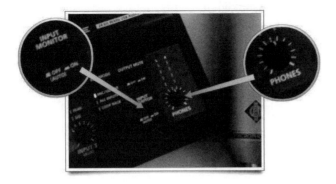

Figure 10.9. Roland Tri-Capture

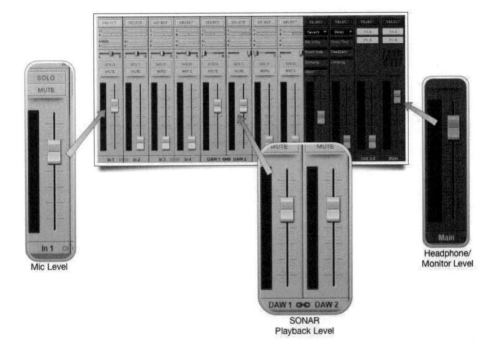

Figure 10.10. PreSonus AudioBox 44VSL mixer app

Interfaces, such as the Octa-Capture, support enough inputs to record an entire band. Because they have multiple outputs, you can actually configure different mixes for different artists, by using the mixer app. It is beyond the scope of this book to go into these details. The approach varies by audio interface model. Note: If you want to set up additional headphone mixes, you will usually need add-on headphone amps for each additional stereo mix.

There are two situations where you will use Input Echo. The first is when recording with a guitar amp simulator, such as TH2, and the second is when recording with Soft Synths.

Setting Recording Levels and Meters

My strategy while recording in SONAR is to get the track meter to peak at about half of the full scale. While recording, there is no advantage to pushing the meters into the red. Modern gear, 24-bit recording has plenty of extra dynamic range; you don't need to push it! Most of us are using affordable audio interfaces, but not necessarily super high-end. The lower-costing gear sounds great as long as you keep the signal well below full scale, where it overloads and distorts.

As I record, I keep the peak level 12 dB below full scale. This gives me plenty of headroom for the transients that sneak past, while staying well below the level that produces nasty overload artifacts. I set up the record meters directly on the track in a particular way, which we'll explore next.

1. Open the Track Control Manager, create a new preset, and name it "Record." In the Audio Strip column, enable Input, Output, MSR, and Edit Filter.

Widget Section	Audio Strip
Vol	☐
Pan	☐
Gain	☐
Input	☑
Output	☑
FX	☐
Aux	☐
Input Gain	☐
Input Pan	☐
MIDI Channel	☐
Bank	☐
Patch	☐
MSR	☑
Track State	☐
Edit Filter	☑

Figure 10.11. Record setup

Choose this configuration when recording for a very concise track strip.

Figure 10.12. Customized record track strip

2. Next, let's make the meters horizontal. On the Track view menu, navigate to Options > Meter Options and select Horizontal Meters. While there, match the other settings to those in Fig. 10.13 as well. Modern computer screens don't have much vertical height, but they do have lots of horizontal width.

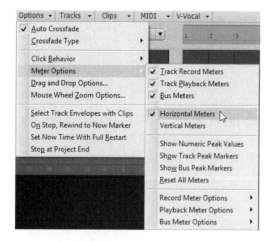

Figure 10.13. Meter options

3. For digital recording, I prefer to monitor by using peak meter focused settings in the upper portion of the scale. To set this up, navigate to the Track view menu > Options > Meter Options > Record Meter Options and select Peak and −24dB.

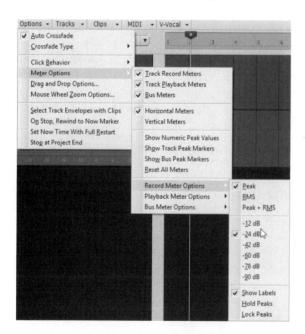

Figure 10.14. Setting the Record Meter scale and range

Tip: If you record with the meters set this way, make sure to keep the peaks near the middle of the meter, you will get a nice, strong signal with very little risk of overloading the input. The result? Great-quality recordings!

Recording with your levels near the middle of the scale affords you a great deal of headroom for transients. If you feel your waveforms on screen look too wimpy this way, adjust the view by dragging up or down on the audio scale.

Figure 10.15. Peaks centered during recording

Note: You can adjust the meter response in the Preferences Dialog on the very last page, named Audio Meter. If you don't see it, check the bottom of the Preferences Dialog to make sure the checkbox for the Advanced selection is checked. I tend to customize these settings. Figure 10.16 shows how I had them set at the time of writing.

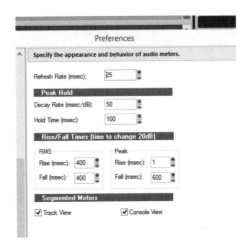

Figure 10.16. Global Audio Meter preferences

Customizing the track strip this this way gives you exactly what you need during recording.

Adjusting the Waveform Height

Properly recorded audio waveforms tend to look wimpy in SONAR (and other DAWs) unless you zoom up the vertical size of the waveform. One day I hope we can set a default waveform magnification, but for now it's easy enough to adjust the view by dragging the audio scale up or down by dragging up or down on the Audio Scale Ruler or on any track. A double click will reset it.

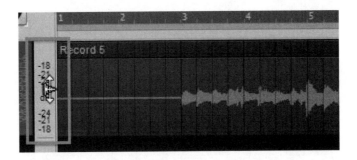

Figure 10.17. Adjusting the waveform height

Overdubbing to a New Track

Overdubbing is recording while listening to previously recorded tracks. This is a key music production technique that allows you to double parts, have one singer sing several harmony parts, or let one songwriter play every instrument on a demo.

To overdub in SONAR, set up a new track configured for the correct instrument or mic and arm it for recording. A quick way to create a new track is to clone an existing track by using Clone Track from the right-click menu. In the Clone Track dialog box, deselect Clone Events and press OK. This will set up a new track with exactly the same settings but without copying over any recorded audio.

Figure 10.18. Cloning a track without events

Make sure to disable Record on the earlier track, so that you don't record over your previous track. Next, enable Record on the new track. Rewind (W), then hit Record (R) and lay down the second part. If the first part is distracting, turn down the volume or mute it.

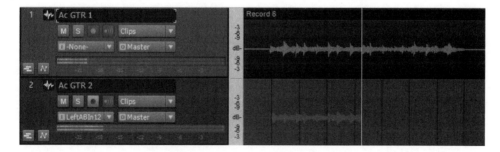

Figure 10.19. Overdubbing to a parallel track

Many songs are recorded entirely by overdubbing track by track. You can also overdub to enhance full band recordings or live stage recordings.

Recording Several Inputs at Once

When you record with several mics or instruments at once, the mechanics remain the same. You need to configure the input for each track with a separate physical input from your audio interface. Have the musicians do a sound check so you can best adjust the input levels.

The biggest challenge is to set up monitoring for the musicians, so that while recording they can hear the existing tracks, the other musicians, and themselves. As I mentioned before, the monitor mix is usually set up outside SONAR by using the software app for the audio interface or an external mixer.

Recording to Takes

Before the X2 version, SONAR tracks had "layers." Since X2, layers have been renamed "takes." This goes along with other features to build composite tracks from multiple overdubbed takes.

If you want several takes of the same part, it works best to record by using different takes recorded to a single track. The advantage is that as you build up new takes, you can easily try out the alternative takes one at a time, using the exclusive solo feature. Later, you can use various parts of different takes to build a composite of the best musical phrases.

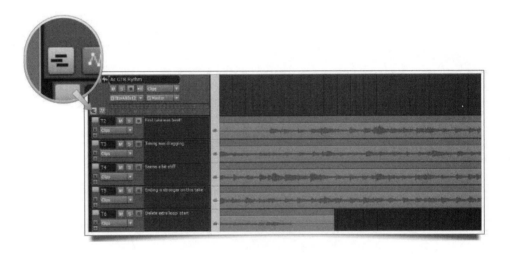

Figure 10.20. Take lanes

Using Take Lanes is always optional, but it can be an efficient and organized way to manage tracking sessions once you get the hang of it. You might think Take Lanes as a tool for loop recording, but I rarely use them that way. They are great way for organizing multiple takes of a part, even if you aren't doing any loop recording.

Takes appear in SONAR under and indented from the parent audio track. They have different track strip controls, compared to the parent track. Let's go over the essentials for using Take Lanes:

Set the Record Mode. Right-click on the Record button in the Control Bar to jump to the Record page in the Preferences dialog box (P). Make sure the Record Mode is set to "Sound on Sound (Blend)." You should also select Store Takes in a Single Track and Create New Lanes on Overlap.

Figure 10.21. Preferences Setting for Using Takes

Here are the key track strip controls for using takes:

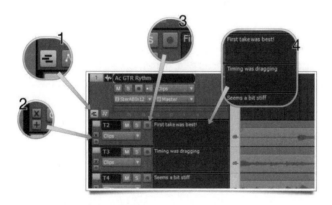

Figure 10.22. Track strip for takes

1. **Expand/Collapse Take Lanes.** Click the Takes button (Shift + T) to see all available take lanes for a track.
2. **Add/Remove Take Lanes.** Each take has an Add button (labeled with a plus sign [+]), and a Remove button (labeled with an X). The Add button will add a new take lane at the bottom, whereas the remove lanes button will delete a specific take.
3. **Record.** Arm the take and record as you normally would. Add additional takes for each addition overdub pass for that track.
4. **Add Take Comments.** Each take track strip has a comments area on the right. Double-click the Comments area and type in useful details about that particular take.

During playback, simply select the take you want to use for the track. You can also click the Takes button to hide all the takes when you aren't working on them.

I will go over creating a composite (called comping) from Take Lanes when we explore editing later in the book.

Loop Recording to Takes

To loop record to take lanes, enable looping (L) and record to a track. When the recording reaches the loop end marker, SONAR will loop back and start a new take on a new take lane.

Here is how to set up and use the loop recording function:

1. **Set Up the Loop.** Toggle the Loop On/Off button in the Loop module or use shortcut L. Draw in the range you want to loop on the timeline by making a selection, then clicking the Set Loop Points button (Shift +L).

Figure 10.23. Setting the loop for loop recording

2. **Set the Loop Recording Mode.** Right-click on the Record button in the Control Bar to jump to the Record page in the Preferences dialog box. Select the "Store Takes in a Single Track" option and verify that the Record Mode is set to "Sound on Sound (Blend)," as I noted earlier.

3. **Record.** Arm the track for recording and record as many passes through the loop as you want. Hit the space bar to stop recording.

4. **Expand the Take Lanes.** Click the Takes button on the track strip to show all the takes if they aren't already visible.

5. **Exclusive Solo.** During playback, you will hear all the takes at once. Solo each one to audition them one at a time. Leave the one you like best soloed. You can also just mute and unmute the clips by using the Mute tool, though I prefer to just solo the best takes.

Those are the essentials for loop recording. Later, we will cover how to build a composite from the various takes.

Recording with a Guitar Amp Simulator

SONAR X2 Producer is bundled with an excellent guitar amp simulator—Overloud's TH2. Lots of excellent third-party amp simulators are on the market as well, including Waves GTR, IK AmpliTube, NI Guitar Rig, Scuffham S-Gear, and Studio Devil Amp Modeler Pro. All of these are used as insert plug-ins while recording.

> **Tip:** To hear the amp processing while recording, make sure to turn on Input echo for the track and turn off any direct monitoring from your audio interface or mixer.

Following are the steps to record with the TH2—note that the process is essentially the same as with any other amp simulator:

1. Create a mono track and assign it the input to which your guitar is connected. I suggest using the Instrument input on your audio interface. Guitars typically have very high impedance, and though plugging them into a standard line level input might work, your tone will suffer. Choose the input designed for guitars.

Figure 10.24. TH2 recording setup

2. Insert TH2, or your other amp simulator plug-in, to the track you just created. I prefer to drag it from the Plug-ins tab of the Browser to the FX bin, using the Inspector pane or Console view.

3. Turn on Input echo and test the signal level. Select a preset and tweak the sound to find a great guitar tone.

   Note: Because you are monitoring through the software, there will be some degree of latency. You will probably want to lower the ASIO buffer setting to get the lowest latency, while still getting clean playback. There is always a balancing act between having low latency and stable playback when recording using amp simulator plugins.

4. Arm the track and record as you normally would. Remember, you are only recording the dry guitar signal. The amp sim effect is created in real time, which means you can tweak the guitar sound during playback, even after completing your recording. You can switch to a different preset or even to a completely different amp sim plug-in!

In this chapter we covered a wide range of audio recording scenarios. The best way to master these techniques is to practice recording. When you have captured some cool tracks, it's time to start editing!

Chapter 11
EDITING AUDIO

E diting audio in SONAR is all about working with clips. Cutting, moving, looping, trimming, fading in, fading out, stretching, and correcting timing are all possible. This chapter introduces the tools and techniques used for audio editing in SONAR.

Smart Tool

As of SONAR X2, the Smart tool has been optimized so you rarely need to switch tools, which saves a lot of unnecessary keystrokes and mouse clicking. In this book, most of the editing described can be done without switching tools.

When you do need to switch tools, use the buttons in the Tools module on the Control Bar. Alternatively, pick tools from the Tools Heads Up Display (HUD), which pulls up the buttons from the Tools module near the mouse pointer. Click T to access the Tools HUD. As soon as you select a tool, the HUD disappears.

Figure 11.1. Tools Heads Up Display

Basic Editing

Since SONAR X2 came out, I do 95 percent of my editing with the Smart tool. Make sure the Smart tool (F5) is selected to try out these techniques. Most editing will follow the current Snap to Grid setting, which we will learn more about shortly. If you want to experiment with editing, turn Snap to Grid off for now, by using the button in the Snap module or keyboard shortcut N.

Here are the basic editing actions:

Selecting Clips

Select a clip by clicking on it with the Smart tool. If you click in the body of the clip, it will also position the cursor (and Now Time) to that spot. If you click on the header, the clip will be selected, but the cursor will not follow. Selected clips appear in a bright highlighted color scheme.

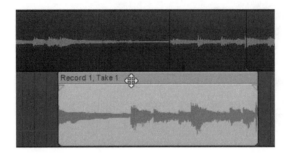

Figure 11.2. A selected clip

Selecting a Range

To select a range, start the selection within the body of the clip and drag right or left. The mouse pointer will appear as an I-beam selector. To extend the selection across multiple tracks, drag down or up across the other tracks.

Figure 11.3. Selecting a range

Lasso Select

You can lasso selections by dragging while holding down the right mouse button. All the clips touched by the lasso area will be selected. This is great for making selections within a crowded project.

Figure 11.4. Lasso select

Moving Clips

To move a clip, drag it forward or backward by grabbing the clip header. You can also move a clip to another track by dragging it from the header area. To prevent the timing from changing, hold down the Shift key as you drag it to a different track. Holding down Shift constrains the timing and keeps your clips in perfect sync when moving from track to track.

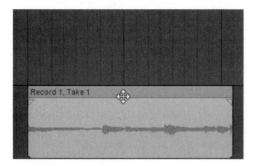

Figure 11.5. Moving a clip

Copying Clips

To copy a clip, hold Ctrl as you drag the clip within a track or from track to track. Hold down Ctrl + Shift as you drag to copy and constrain the timing when moving it to a new track. Normal Windows cut, copy, and paste functions work as well. Select a clip, then use Ctrl + C to copy or Ctrl + X to cut. Select the destination track, position the cursor at the new time, and use Ctrl + V to paste the clip.

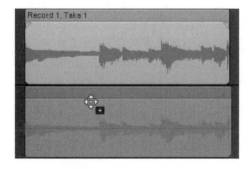

Figure 11.6. Copying a clip

Splitting Clips

To split a clip, hold down the Alt key and position the cursor over the clip header. The mouse pointer will appear as the split tool. Click where you want to make the split. If you have clips selected across several tracks, they will all split. Alternatively, you can position the cursor to where the split should happen and hit the S key.

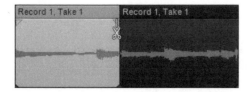

Figure 11.7. Splitting clips

Slip-Editing Clips

To adjust the length of a clip, drag the beginning or ending edge inward. The mouse pointer will appear as a left–right arrow when positioned correctly. The SONAR manual calls this slip-editing, but other software calls it trimming or resizing.

Figure 11.8. Slip-editing clips (trimming)

Note that you can also use the Select tool (F6), the Move tool (F7), and the Split tool (F8). However, there is usually no advantage to this approach, unless you are already used to it. The Smart tool, along with the modifiers, consolidates all these actions in a very efficient and elegant way.

Fades and Crossfades

It is easy to add fades to the beginning or ending of a clip. To add a fade-in, position your cursor in the upper left corner of the clip, just below the clip header. The mouse pointer will appear as a triangle. Drag it right to create the fade-in. For fade-outs, do the same thing, but start from the upper right corner and drag it to the left.

Figure 11.9. Creating a fade-in

Once a fade is in place, you can adjust the position by dragging the red triangle. To remove the fade, drag the red triangle back to the edge of the clip. You can also select the shape of the fade envelope by right-clicking on the fade handle and selecting one of the three shapes from the list.

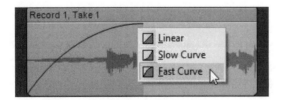

Figure 11.10. Fade shapes selection

You can crossfade from one clip to the next using fade-ins and fadeouts, as I just described. However, it's much faster to enable Auto Crossfade from the Track view menu, under Options > Auto Crossfade. Enabling it allows the fade-ins and -outs to be created automatically if you overlap clips.

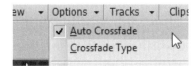

Figure 11.11. Turning on Auto Crossfade

With Auto Crossfade enabled, fades are created automatically when you overlap clips. Note: Auto Crossfade only works if you have the option "Blend Old and New" set in the Preferences dialog box on the Editing page.

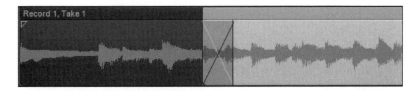

Figure 11.12. Auto Crossfade example

Crossfades are useful when editing and can reduce clicks and pops—making transitions seamless. To control the default shapes for fades and crossfades, navigate to the settings under Options > Crossfade Type on the Track view menu.

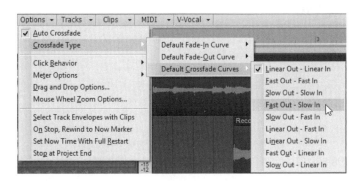

Figure 11.13. Crossfade types

Aim Assist

Aim Assist is a dotted, vertical line that follows your mouse pointer around in Track view. It helps you visually align clips to the timeline, to other tracks, or to note events in MIDI tracks. As of X2, it is turned on by default. You can turn it on or off by navigating to Edit > Aim Assist or keyboard shortcut X. It's a great aid for editing.

If you drag a clip with Aim Assist enabled, the vertical line moves to the edge of the clip and serves as a guide. If you drag from the left half of the clip, the line will be positioned at the left edge; if you drag a clip from the right half, the line will be positioned to the right. Although this function is really helpful, it can be confusing if you don't know why the line is sometimes to the right.

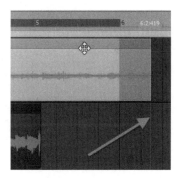

Figure 11.14. Aim Assist

Snap to Grid

Snap to Grid is an essential tool for aligning clips to musical time during editing. With Snap to Grid turned on, clips will snap into place and align to the nearest grid increment as you move them. The grid affects many actions in SONAR besides controlling clip timing. It is also used when positioning the Now Time cursor, drawing in fades, and using aim assist. Most snap options are found in the Snap module on the Control Bar. Since SONAR X2, there is a cool new Smart Grid mode that adjusts the grid increments based on the zoom level.

Here are the key things you need to know about snap:

1. **Turning Snap to Grid On/Off.** Use keyboard shortcut N or the Snap module button to toggle Snap to Grid on or off.

Figure 11.15. Snap module controls

2. **Snap By.** Normally, you will want to leave this switch in the Snap To position. This means that the beginnings of clips will snap to the nearest grid increment during moves and copies. Use Snap By to drag a clip to a new location in time if the original didn't start correctly on a grid division. Other DAWs call this relative snap. For example, a chorus vocal phase starts with a pickup a bit ahead of the downbeat. Now you want to drag the clip to the second chorus. Set the grid to Snap By then Ctrl-drag the clip to new chorus. The clip will fall at the same place relative to the new downbeat with the pickup properly ahead of the downbeat.

3. **Grid Settings.** To set the musical divisions for the snap grid, right-click on the grid button in the Snap module. From here, you can pick common music time values, such as whole, quarter, or eighth notes. There are also options for ticks, samples frames, or seconds. Those are useful in situations when working with video, voiceover, or freely recorded music. Next to the main grid settings button, you will find modifier buttons for applying triplet and dotted timing to the grid.

4. **Smart Grid.** To enable the Smart Grid, click menu at the top of the Grid Settings menu. This is new as of X2. With Smart Grid turned on, the grid will adjust to the best musical time value to match the current zoom level. For example, if you zoom out, the grid may show as full measures; but if you zoom in to show five bars of music, the grid will adjust to sixteenth notes. This can save you the effort of having to adjust the grid every time you change the zoom level.

5. **Dotted or Triplet Grid.** To the right of the main grid settings button, you will find modifier buttons to apply dotted or triplet timing. You can add one or the other, or leave them both off for straight time.

6. **Snap to Landmark Events.** In addition to snapping strictly to the grid, SONAR allows snapping to other types of events or landmarks. By default, Snap to Landmarks is off, but you can enable this by clicking on the button resembling a mountain with a flag in the Snap module. To see the available types of landmarks, right-click the Snap to Landmark Events button and open the Preferences dialog box for the settings. I've found the most useful of these to be snapping to other clips and the Now Time. Most of the time, I leave Snap to Landmark Events turned off.

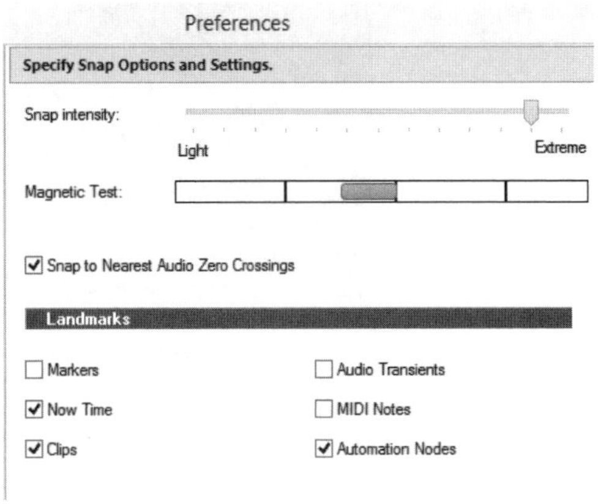

Figure 11.16. Snap to Landmark options

Snap Intensity. Snapping could be described as a magnetic in SONAR. As you drag a clip near a grid line, the magnetic pull draws the clip into place. You can adjust the magnetic strength by adjusting the Snap intensity in the Preference dialog box on the Snap to Grid page. This page also holds the Snap to Landmark settings (Figure 11.16). I usually adjust it toward the more extreme end of the scale, but try out lighter settings if you would like more flexibility in placing clips somewhat off the grid without overriding the snap.

Secondary Snap Setup. If you hold down the N key, SONAR switches to an entire secondary Snap setup. As you hold N, change any of the snap setup options to be remembered as your secondary setup. To use the secondary setup, just hold down N. I often like to keep the main snap setting at whole notes and configure the secondary to sixteenth notes. You can also leave the main snap setup on Smart Snap and apply the secondary setup to whole notes to easily move song sections around.

Groove Clip Loops— Drag and Drop Instant Gratification

Drag a loop file to a track from the Media browser. It will appear on the track as a clip with rounded corners; this is called a Groove clip. When you drag the right edge of a Groove clip to the right, you can roll out endless copies, making it easy to paint something like a drumbeat across a song section or entire tune.

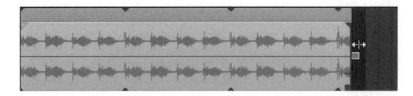

Figure 11.17. Rolling out a Groove Clip loop

You can easily convert any clip to a Groove Clip by selecting it and pressing Ctrl + L. Additional properties are available in the Groove Clip section of the Clip Properties in the Inspector pane. There you will find properties to enable or disable looping, as well as a value to set number of beats in the loop.

Although it is beyond the scope of this book, you can control detailed aspects of Groove clips by using the Loop Construction view, which opens in the MultiDock. By default, double-clicking an audio clip will open this view. You can also find it from in the Menu under Views > Loop Construction (Alt + 7).

Figure 11.18. Groove Clip Properties in the Inspector

AudioSnap

SONAR has the amazing ability to stretch audio clips, effectively allowing you to mash-up unrelated beats or correct for timing errors. AudioSnap is a complex feature, but we'll explore the essentials to get you started.

AudioSnap allows you warp or quantize audio without chopping it up into discrete beats and hits. This editing technique is based on detecting transients (the front edge of a note) and then either dragging the transients by hand, or else by quantizing them (matching them to musical note divisions). AudioSnap can also be used to quantize multitrack drums, but in this example, I will use a simple stereo drum part.

Here are the basic steps to apply AudioSnap:

Select the track to work with and use the Edit Filter in the track strip to select Audio Transients. This automatically enables AudioSnap and detects the transients.

Figure 11.19. Selecting audio transients in the Edit Filter

Note: You can open an AudioSnap palette by pressing the A key. Use the Enable AudioSnap button to disable or enable AudioSnap for the selected tracks. You can also enable or disable it in the AudioSnap section found in the Clip Properties tab of the Inspector.

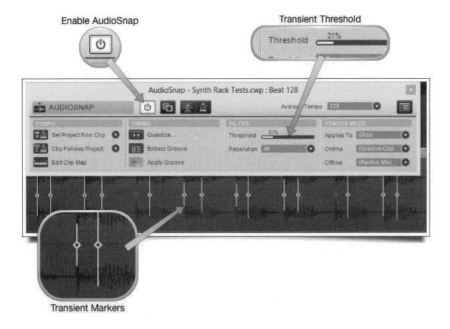

Enable AudioSnap

Transient Threshold

Threshold 21%

Transient Markers

Figure 11.20. AudioSnap palette

With AudioSnap enabled, you will see transient markers indicated. Look at the clip and judge how well weaker transients are being picked up, then adjust the Threshold slider until it is picking up all the notes, while rejecting false transients.

Working with Transient Markers

Now that you have transient markers detected and visible, you can use them to edit the audio in simple but powerful ways. Use the Smart tool for all of these examples.

Adjust Timing Manually. Grab the upper or lower "line" part of a transient marker and drag it to where you want to start the note. The audio will stretch between the other markers and can be easily lined up to the grid or other notes and drum hits. I prefer leaving Snap off for most of this type of editing.

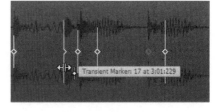

Figure 11.21. Adjust timing

Moving Transient Markers. Grab any transient marker from the center and align it just ahead of the transient relative to the waveform. This allows you to correctly place transients that appear a bit off from the automatic detection.

Deleting Transient Markers. To delete a transient marker, first select it, then hit Delete on your keyboard. To delete several at once, highlight them and hit Delete.

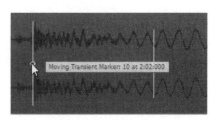

Figure 11.22. Moving transient markers

These few tools are enough to get you started using AudioSnap. As you drag transient markers, you will find they snap to the current grid setting. If are trying to line things up to another audio part while you edit, try turning Snap off.

Note: AudioSnap uses a different, more efficient, algorithm during playback than it does while rendering. The audio quality suffers a bit when using AudioSnap, but when you export the mix or bounce the track, the offline processing sounds better. You can set both the real-time and offline algorithms in the AudioSnap palette (A).

AudioSnap Quantizing

You can use AudioSnap to automatically quantize transients to a music function. This process works very much the same as manual quantizing.

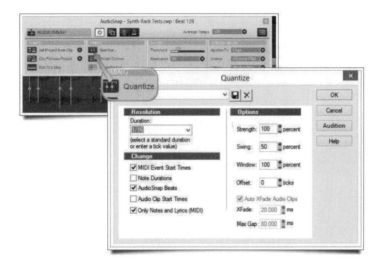

Figure 11.23. AudioSnap quantizing

After you have detected the transient markers, use the AudioSnap palette (A) and click on Quantize to load the Quantize dialog box. Select the Quantize resolution and parameters and click OK. This will automatically adjust the transient markers throughout the track to line up with the chosen resolution. If you don't like the results, undo (Ctrl + Z), and try again!

When you are finished using AudioSnap, hide the transient markers by changing the Edit Filter setting back to clips.

Editing with Groups

There are various reasons to edit several clips together. The best example is when you don't want clips from one drum mic to move relative to the other mics while editing multitrack drums. Fortunately, you can easily group clips before editing them to keep them in sync. When grouped, you only need to edit one of the clips, and the edits will apply to all the others.

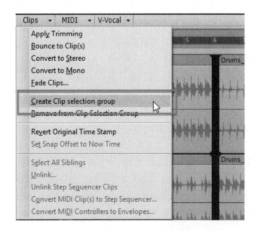

Figure 11.24. Creating a clip selection group

To create a clip group, select some clips using the Smart tool, then select "Create selection group from selected clips" from the right-click menu. You can also access it from the Track view menu under Clips. Any edits to a clip group, such as the split shown in Figure 11.25, will apply to all the clips in the group.

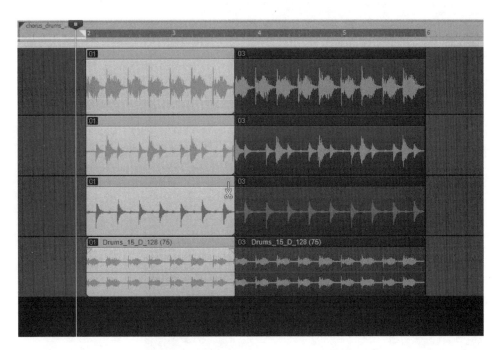

Figure 11.25. Splitting drums using a clip group

Comping

In the previous chapter on recording audio, we explored how to record takes. You can do this directly or by loop recording. Either way, I suggest converting all these takes into a best take by making a composite of the best phrases across takes. There is a special technique for selecting the best phrases from takes in SONAR. In music production, this is called comping.

There are several ways to build the composite, but here is what I believe to be the most efficient way in SONAR:

1. Expand the takes using the Takes button on the track strip.

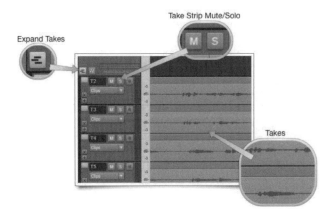

Figure 11.26. Expanding the takes

2. Set up a loop over the first phrase of the part.
3. Select the Mute tool from the Command Bar Tools module. If it's not shown, right-click the Erase tool and select Mute.

Figure 11.27. Switching to the Mute tool

4. Ctrl-swipe the first phrase on the first take to audition the phrase. This action mutes the phrase in all the other takes leaving your selection as the only one that will play back. Use the same Ctrl-swipe technique to audition the same phrase in the other takes. Leave your favorite take playing back.

Tip: The Mute tool Ctrl-swipe selection of phrases is the key to comping in SONAR.

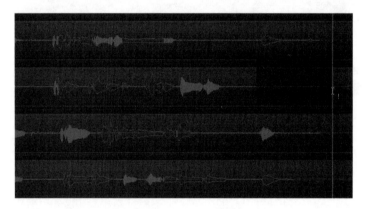

Figure 11.28. Ctrl-swipe with the Mute tool

5. Next, set the loop over the next phrase and repeat the audition/selection process using Ctrl-swipe with the Mute tool. Continue this process until you have worked through the entire part.
6. With the composite selections finished, switch back to the Smart tool. Close the takes then freeze the track, using the Freeze button on the track strip. Now you have a completed composite track! If you want to make changes to the comp track, unfreeze the track, open the takes, and update your phrase selections, using the Mute tool.

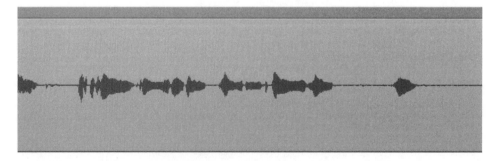

Figure 11.29. The completed composite track

Those are the essential tools and techniques you need to edit audio in SONAR. Now it's time to explore the MIDI and Soft Synths. Let's move on and learn about an entirely different approach to making music with SONAR!

Chapter 12
RECORDING WITH SOFT SYNTHS

In this chapter, we'll explore Soft Synths and MIDI recording. Soft Synths are often called virtual instruments in the world of digital audio recording. They can be a little tricky to work with, but SONAR makes it easy once you understand the basics. SONAR Producer has numerous Soft Synths, including Dimension Pro, z3ta+, and SessionDrummer, among others. Each one has its own unique interface and collection of sounds, but the steps to adding one to your project are the same.

I will be using Dimension Pro for these examples. Dimension Pro is a sample-based Soft Synth that covers a full range of sounds—from natural instruments to unnatural special effects. You can expand the palette of sounds by selecting from a wide variety of add-on sound packs from the Cakewalk Store.

Because this is an introduction, I will focus on using Simple Instrument Tracks, which combine a MIDI recording, a Soft Synth, and a stereo output channel into a single entity. We will cover multitimbral Soft Synths and multioutput drum instruments in a later chapter.

Adding a Simple Instrument Track

To add a Soft Synth your project, open the Browser and click the Synth tab. If you don't see the Browser, just click B to open it.

Click the "Insert Synth" button to open the list of all your plug-in Soft Synths. After you select a Soft Synth, the Insert Soft Synths Options Dialog Box will come up. In this instance, choose "Simple Instrument Track." After you click OK, an instrument track is created within a few seconds and the Soft Synth appears in the Synth Rack.

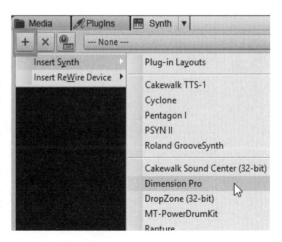

Figure 12.1. Adding a Soft Synth to the Synth Rack

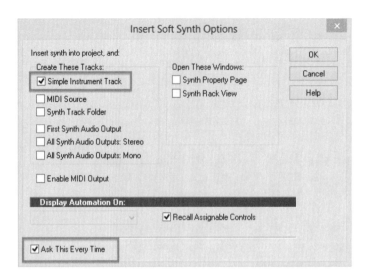

Figure 12.2. Insert Soft Synths options

At bottom of the Insert Soft Synth Options dialog box, you can turn off "Ask This Every Time" by clearing the checkbox. This can improve workflow if you mostly work with Simple Instrument tracks. You can always change these options from the Insert Synth Options button on the Synth tab.

A Simple Instrument Track is easy to understand, because it holds MIDI clips and is assigned to one Soft Synth in the Synth Rack. Furthermore, there is one Console channel that corresponds to the Simple Instrument track.

Select a Soft Synth Sound

Double-click the track type icon to open the window for the Soft Synth—in this case, Dimension Pro. Play a few notes on your MIDI keyboard controller. You should be able to hear sound from SONAR.

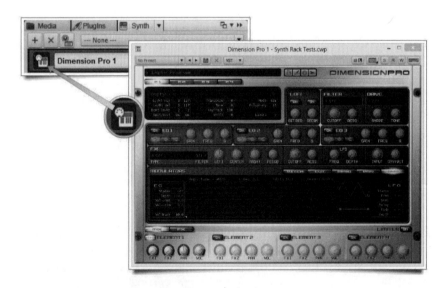

Figure 12.3. Opening the Soft Synth window

To audition sounds in Dimension Pro, select the category and sound from the patch browser. This may differ slightly with another Soft Synth. In this example, I selected a bass sound.

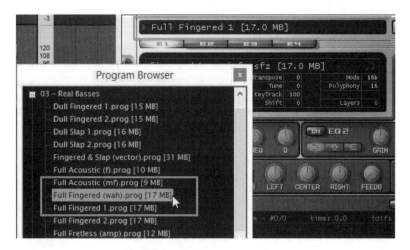

Figure 12.4. Selecting a bass patch on Dimension Pro

Recording a MIDI Part

Now with the Instrument track created, I added an audio track with a simple drum Groove clip loop and rolled it out over several bars to create some rhythm to work with while recording. I usually find this more inspiring than just listening to the metronome click.

At this point, recording a MIDI performance is just like recording audio—arm the track for recording, rewind, hit Record, and play in the part. You arm the track with the Record button on the track strip, rewind with W, or the transport RTZ button, and start recording with R, or the Record button on the Transport module.

If you want a count-in, set it up in the Metronome settings in the Options dialog box. I usually set "Record Count In" to two measures to give myself some time to feel the tempo before recording. When you've finished recording the part, turn off Record Enable for that track.

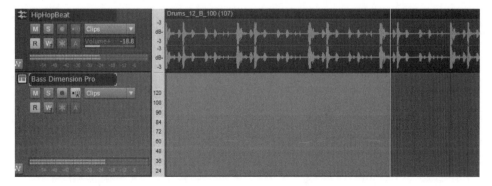

Figure 12.5. MIDI recording in process

Note: During recording and playback, keep Input Echo enabled on Instrument tracks or you won't hear sound from the Soft Synth.

Soft Synths and Latency

The sound of Soft Synths comes from your computer and its CPU power. Fundamentally, SONAR acts as a host for the Soft Synth. If you are playing a Soft Synth from a USB MIDI Controller, you want a very responsive and immediate experience. This means you don't want a delay between playing notes on your controller and hearing the notes come out of your speakers.

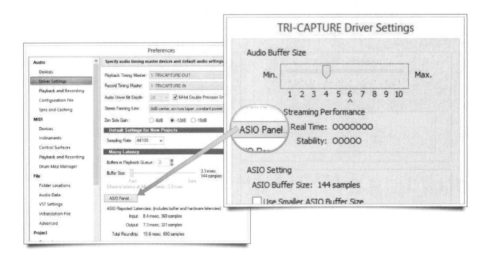

Figure 12.6. Preferences latency settings

Latency, typically measured in milliseconds, is the time your computer needs to calculate the mix of everything in your project before you hear it. Most musicians won't feel a latency of a few dozen milliseconds. One to 30 ms of latency is barely noticeable. However, if it's 60 ms or more, it starts to get noticeable or even annoying. If it's too high, it can throw off your timing and kill a performance.

When recording MIDI, you will want to tune the latency settings of your system to be as low as possible without becoming glitchy. This sort of balancing act is one of the trickiest things about computer music making. It really helps to have a powerful computer with four or more cores and 8 GB or more of memory. You can also Freeze tracks you have completed, as described in the next section.

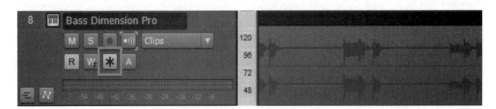

Figure 12.7. Track Freeze button

MIDI Track Freeze

A simple way to unload your computer CPU and keep your latency settings low is to use the Freeze button on the instrument tracks you have finished. This mixes the MIDI clips to audio, using the sound of the Soft Synth, and takes them offline. If your project is starting to bog down, Freeze some of the tracks you aren't working on. You can reverse the Freeze at any time by hitting the button again.

X-Ray Windows

Soft Synth windows take up a lot of space on the screen. You might find yourself shuffling and closing them to work with the underlying tracks, which can waste a lot of time. This is where the SONAR's X-Ray comes in.

With any Soft Synth open, press Shift + X. This toggles on the X-Ray mode. Now the Soft Synth windows still shown, but it is transparent so you can see and work with the tracks behind it. To switch this back, hit Shift + X again. This is a great function for when you are going back and forth between MIDI editing and tweaking a synth sound.

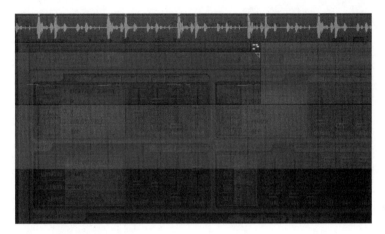

Figure 12.8. X-Ray Windows

There are a few configuration options for X-Ray Windows available in the Preferences dialog box (P) on the Display tab. Here, you can disable the feature entirely and set the Fade In/Out times in milliseconds. The most important parameter here is the Opacity percentage, which sets the amount of transparency to match your screen and preference.

Figure 12.9. Display options for X-Ray in the Preferences dialog box

Chapter 13

EDITING MIDI

There are several ways to work with MIDI notes once you have a performance recorded to an Instrument track or MIDI track. You can edit MIDI clips similarly to audio clips. The real power in SONAR is working with the individual MIDI notes in the Piano Roll view (PRV). SONAR also supports an inline PRV, a Staff view, and the classic Event List view.

Editing MIDI Clips in Track View

When you record Soft Synth performances, MIDI notes data is recorded to MIDI clips in Track view. A MIDI clip acts as a container for MIDI notes, making it easier to move groups of notes and phrases without treating them as separate events.

MIDI clips appear on Instrument tracks and MIDI tracks and can be identified by the MIDI clip icon in the upper right corner. A typical MIDI clip also shows MIDI notes in a view-only representation, rather than an audio waveform.

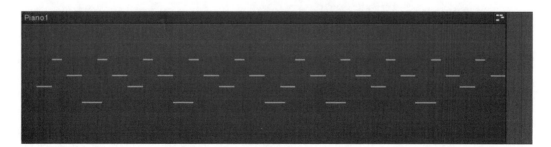

Figure 13.1. A MIDI clip

The MIDI tracks show a MIDI scale at the left—representing MIDI note numbers rather than the dB scale seen for audio tracks. You can adjust the data zoom level by dragging down on the time scale. A useful trick is to right-click the MIDI scale and select Fit Content to optimize the view and center it around the actual notes present on the track.

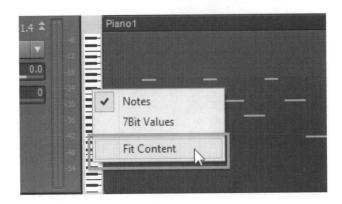

Figure 13.2. Adjusting the MIDI scale

Just as with audio clips, you can use the Smart tool for most operations. Much of what we've already covered about audio editing also applies to MIDI clips, so this may seem like a review.

Let's explore the most common things you need to know about working with MIDI clips.

Selecting MIDI Clips

Select a MIDI clip by clicking on it with the Smart tool. If you click in the body of the clip, it will also position the Now Time cursor to that spot. If you click on the clip header, you can select the clip without changing moving the cursor. Selected clips are highlighted with a bright background.

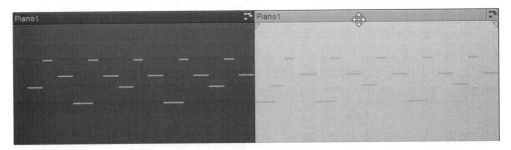

Figure 13.3. Selecting a clip

Selecting a Range

To select a range, start the selection within the body of the clip and drag right or left. The mouse pointer will appear as an I-beam tool. Drag right or left to select a range within a track; drag up or down to extend the selection across tracks. A range select can even be a mix of audio clips and MIDI clips.

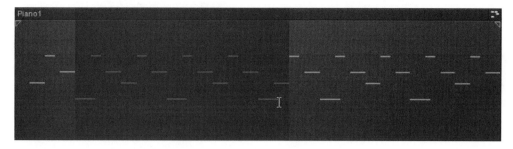

Figure 13.4. Selecting a range on a MIDI clip

Lasso Select

Lasso select by dragging while holding down the right mouse button. The full clip will be selected for all clips touched by the lasso area.

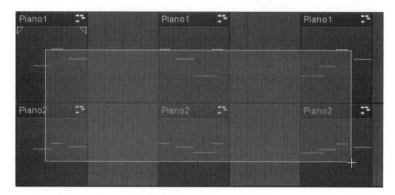

Figure 13.5. Using Lasso select with MIDI clips

Moving Clips

To move a clip, drag it forward or backward by grabbing it from the clip header. You can also move a clip to another track by dragging it from the header area. Hold down the Shift key as you drag it to a different track to keep the timing in sync.

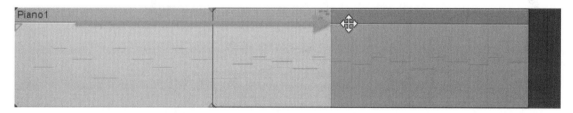

Figure 13.6. Moving a MIDI clip

Copying Clips

To copy a clip, hold down the Ctrl key while dragging the clip within a track or from track to track. To constrain the timing when copying track to track, hold down Ctrl + Shift as you drag. The Windows Cut, Copy, and Paste functions work as well. Select a clip and use Ctrl + C to copy or Ctrl + X to cut. Next, select the destination track, position the cursor, and use Ctrl + V to paste it.

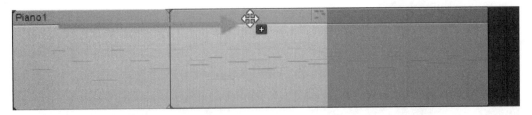

Figure 13.7. Copying a MIDI clip

Splitting Clips

To split a clip, hold down Alt and position the cursor over the clip header. The cursor will appear as the Split tool. Click the spot where you want to split. If you have clips selected across several tracks, they will all split.

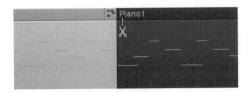

Figure 13.8. Splitting a MIDI clip

Slip-Editing MIDI Clips

To trim or adjust the length of a MIDI clip, drag the beginning edge or the ending edge and drag inward. The mouse pointer will appear as a left–right arrow tool.

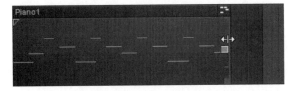

Figure 13.9. Slip-editing a MIDI clip

Editing MIDI Notes in the PRV

Access the PRV by double-clicking a MIDI clip in Track view. You can also right-click the clip and select View > Piano Roll View. Either way, the PRV will open in the MultiDock. The PRV follows a player piano analogy. You see notes organized into a grid with a vertical piano keyboard along the left axis and a time ruler along the top. MIDI notes are positioned in the PRV at the intersection of pitch and time. The note length is also represented graphically. All of this culminates in the MIDI notes being fully represented—what note is played, when in time, and how long it is held. Additional note and controller data is also available, as we will explore shortly. Zooming is handled the same as in Track view. The easiest way is to drag up and down on the Time Ruler.

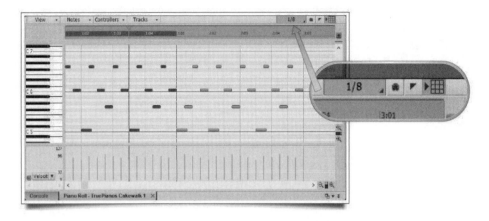

Figure 13.10. Piano Roll View (PRV)

The PRV has its own menu along the top and its own Snap to Grid controls in the upper right. Navigate to View > Show/Hide Controller Pane to display the controllers below the PRV. I think this is a much better way to work with controllers so I leave this pane open.

Figure 13.11. Hide or show the Controller pane

When the Controller pane is closed, the controllers are superimposed on the main PRV. Hide them by clearing Controllers > Select Controllers Along with Notes.

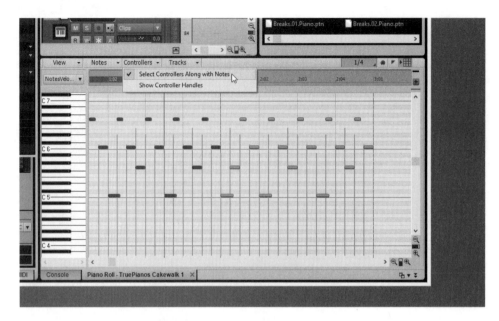

Figure 13.12. Controllers along with notes

With SONAR, most MIDI note editing is done with the Smart tool, just as with clip editing. Actually, editing notes is very similar to editing clips. Most of these operations will respect the current Snap to Grid settings.

Painting Notes. Hold the left mouse button as you paint with the Smart tool to draw in notes on the piano roll. Start dragging from the position where you want the note to play. Drag right to set the note length and up or down to set the note pitch.

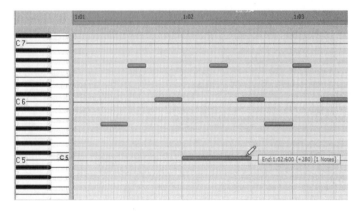

Figure 13.13. Painting notes with the Smart tool

Erasing Notes. Simply right-click a note to erase it. You can also select a note and hit Delete.

Moving Notes. Use the Smart tool to drag notes up or down to change the pitch. Drag notes left or right to change the timing. Notes will snap based on the current Snap to Grid setting.

Splitting Notes. Alt + click to split notes at the Now Time cursor. As you hold down Alt, the mouse pointer appears as a Split tool when over a note. Just click where you want to the split to occur. The split will conform to the current Snap to Grid setting.

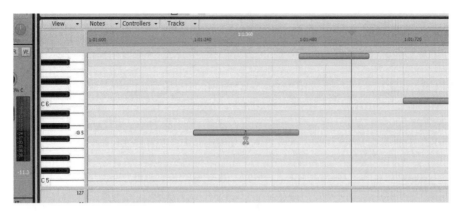

Figure 13.14. Splitting notes with Alt + click

Lasso Selecting Notes. Right-click and drag to draw a lasso selection over a group of notes. Any notes touched by the selection will be fully selected; they don't need to be fully contained in the selection. Once selected, you can move them, delete them, or perform other actions, just like working with a single note.

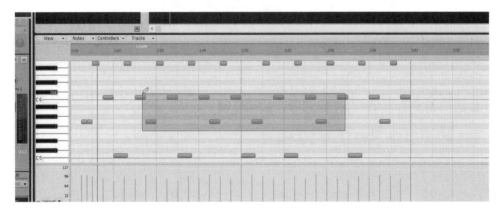

Figure 13.15. Lasso selecting notes with right-drag

Choosing Which Track to Edit. The easiest way is to double-click a MIDI clip in Track view to open the clip for editing it the PRV. If you want to edit more than one track at a time, navigate to Track > Pick Tracks from the PRV menu. Select one or more tracks and PRV will show the notes from all selected tracks in PRV. Use Shift + Ctrl + click to make multiple selections of tracks.

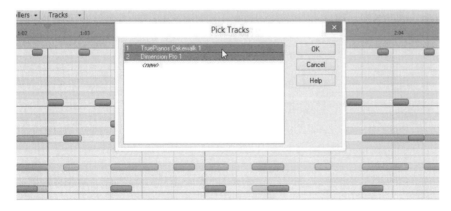

Figure 13.16. Selecting multiple tracks to editing in PRV

Aim Assist in the PRV

I introduced Aim Assist in the editing audio chapter. Aim Assist appears as a vertical guideline to help align clips to the timeline or to other clips. It is enabled globally from Edit > Aim Assist. It is a helpful tool to line up notes from multiple parts and way to tighten the feel of different instruments relative to one another.

For MIDI clips on in the Clips pane, Aim Assist works exactly as it does for audio. Dragging a MIDI note from the left half will make the guideline appear along the beginning of the note; dragging from the right side makes it appear at the ending edge.

For MIDI notes, a horizontal guide also appears to help you position note pitches relative to the virtual piano keyboard.

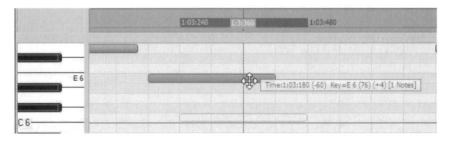

Figure 13.17. Aim Assist in Piano Roll View

Editing Controller Data in Piano Roll View

You can open one or more controller panes at the bottom of the PRV. Each controller pane has its own edit filter, from which you can choose what data is shown. Use the plus icon to add more Controller panes. Use the minus to delete Controller panes.

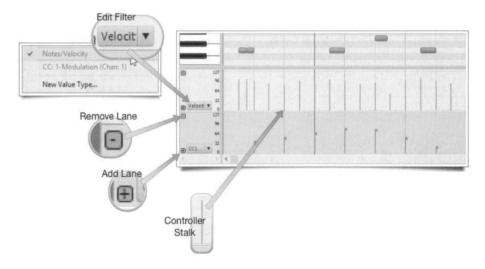

Figure 13.18. Controller pane controls

The controller value is shown as a vertical stalk for any particular note. To change its strength, draw a line across the area you want its value to be set. Click and drag over the controller stalks to paint in controller values. Hold Shift while painting to shape a series of controllers with a straight line.

Tip: It won't work to grab the top of a controller stalk and drag it up and down. Simply draw across it at the level you want to set it.

Using the Inline Piano Roll View

Another way to work with MIDI notes is to open the Inline Piano Roll by selecting "Notes" from the Edit Filter for any MIDI or Instrument track.

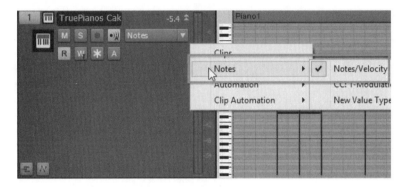

Figure 13.19. Selecting the Inline Piano Roll View

While the features of the Inline Piano Roll are more limited than the full PRV, it can be a cool way to work, especially if you need to visually align MIDI notes to audio.

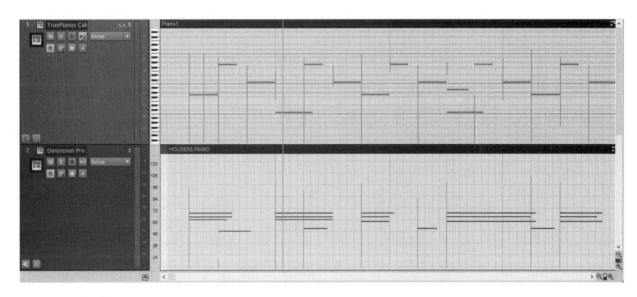

Figure 13.20. Inline PRV

By default, the Inline PRV shows velocity data superimposed over the notes. You can turn this off under the Track view menu by deselecting MIDI > Show Velocity.

Quantizing MIDI Notes

Quantizing MIDI notes is easy and works just like quantizing clips. First, select a series of notes in the PRV using lasso select, or hit Ctrl + A to select all. Press Q to open the Quantize dialog box.

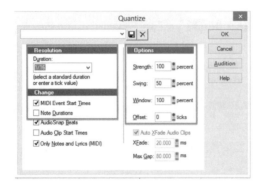

Figure 13.21. Select some notes and press Q to quantize

Set the parameters in the Quantize dialog box and click Audition to hear a sample. Click OK to apply the change. Get your Undo (Ctrl + Z) ready, as quantizing involves some trial and error!

The Quantize dialog box has several parameters that affect the behavior of the action. The parameters outlined in Fig. 13.21 are the values related to MIDI note quantizing. Here is how to use those values.

Duration. This is a drop-down in the Resolution section of the Quantize dialog box. Here, you can set the musical value to use for quantizing, such as whole, 1/8, or 1/16. This is usually the most important setting.

MIDI Event Start Times. Leave this selected to Quantize by adjusting the position of the note start times to match the musical divisions set in Duration above. Most of the time this must set for normal quantizing to work as expected.

Note Durations. Typically, you can leave this off. If you turn this on, note lengths will be quantized, too, which can lead to unnatural or mechanical sounds. Sometimes it can be handy for very sloppy playing!

Strength. Strength sets how far timing is corrected to match the grid. At 100 percent, notes will be snapped perfectly to the grid. If you want to tighten timing without sucking all the feel out the original performance, try easing up on this setting. I find 75 percent to be a very usable value.

> **Tip:** If you ease off on the strength, it's a good idea to listen through the performance and manually correct notes that fall early. This all depends on your style, but is something to be aware of. Notes that fall early tend to sound wrong, whereas notes that fall late sound more expressive.

Swing. Swing sets the amount of syncopation for the off-beats. In practical terms, this means how much the off-beat eighth notes are delayed for the song. If you are quantizing a tune with a syncopated beat and neglect to take this into account, you can quantize the swing feel right out of your song. For a straight time song, leave Swing set to zero.

Note: Another way to quantize with syncopation is to leave it at zero and choose one of the triplet values for the Duration setting; for example, 1/8T or 1/16T.

Tip: If you want to get the feel of the old MPC drum machine swing, try quantizing with Swing set to around 63 percent. I love that feel!

Window. This setting is a bit less obvious. All notes get quantized when Window is set to 100 percent. As you ease off this setting, only notes near the grid are quantized. If you have a busy part with complex fills or percussion, easing off the Windows setting allows you to quantize the strong beats without messing up the rhythm.

Offset. This setting is also not obvious. Offset moves the grid forward or backward, based on ticks. Ticks are the finest level of MIDI timing resolution and are adjustable. Their exact lengths depend on the tempo of the project. Regardless, if you want to layback the timing of a track as you quantize it, put a few ticks in here. I find it can improve the timing of keyboard parts if the musician plays ahead of the beat. I add eight to ten ticks of Offset and set the Strength to 70 percent. This can be very subtle and most SONAR users I know leave Offset at 0 most of the time.

Those are the basics of MIDI editing in SONAR. SONAR has deep foundations as a MIDI sequencer. Beyond this introduction, there are many additional things to explore, such as MIDI FX, Groove Quantize, the Event List, and the Staff view, which are beyond the scope of this book.

Chapter 14

MORE ABOUT SOFT SYNTHS

In the last couple of chapters, I introduced how to set up Instrument tracks and how to record MIDI. We covered the most common scenario—a simple instrument track using one Soft Synth with one stereo output. In this chapter, I will cover other scenarios, including Soft Synths that play several instrument sounds from a single instance and Soft Synths with multiple stereo outputs.

Before we get going, here are a few definitions to help you understand the chapter.

- **Track.** A track is the horizontal representation of a recording along a time ruler in Track view. It is analogous to a one-track on a multitrack tape machine. All modern DAW software is designed this way.

- **Channel.** A channel is the vertical representation of signal flow and includes a volume fader in Console view and the Inspector pane. It is analogous to the channel strip on a mixing console. Multitimbral Soft Synths, such as Cakewalk TTS-1, have their own virtual mixers with multiple channels, so this can get doubly confusing.

- **Instance.** When you load a Soft Synth into the Synth Rack, you create one "instance" of that instrument. Because everything is digital, you can load Dimension Pro four times, for example. Each of those virtual copies of Dimension Pro is an instance of that Soft Synth.

In SONAR, tracks and channels have a one-to-one relationship and are often used interchangeably. This can lead to some confusion, which is why I distinguish between the concepts.

Instrument Tracks vs. MIDI Tracks

There are two different kinds of tracks used to record and arrange MIDI-based music. But what are the differences?

Instrument Tracks. By now, you should be able to set up an Instrument track. An Instrument track brings together a track to record MIDI clips, an instance of a Soft Synth, and a stereo channel in the Console view. The channel and Instrument track have all the capabilities of the audio channel, including the abilities to add plug-in effects and fully access the ProChannel.

MIDI Tracks. MIDI tracks hold MIDI clips, but make no sound on their own. MIDI tracks can be used to drive external hardware sound modules and real-life synthesizers. You can also use them as the source for MIDI notes when setting up multitimbral and multioutput drum Soft Synths.

> **Tip:** Both MIDI tracks and instrument tracks have extra MIDI properties that are accessible from the MIDI tab in the Inspector.

Using Multitimbral Soft Synths

Multitimbral synthesizers can play several different instrument sounds at once. Soft Synths, such as the TTS-1, are modeled after early sound modules, such as the Roland MT-32 and Emu Proteus, which debuted as MIDI devices in the early days of sequencing.

Using a multitimbral Soft Synth, you can use MIDI notes to trigger every sound in an entire song. For example, the TTS-1 covers the all of the most common instrument types, from drums to pianos, and can play up to sixteen different parts at a time. TTS-1 and other similar Soft Synths are a perfect for playing back and working with General MIDI files. General MIDI is an industry standard convention for the layout of instrument sound presets and mapping of drum sounds to MIDI notes.

There are many other third-party multitimbral Soft Synths that support multitimbral setups. Of these, the best known is probably Native Instruments Kontakt—a staple in all kinds of music production that is the engine for all types of sound libraries.

Multitimbral synths are usually set up to play different sounds on each of the sixteen different MIDI channels (not to be confused with Console channels). To use them, create an instrument track for the Soft Synth, as well as the first MIDI part. Next, create a new MIDI track for each additional part you want to trigger from the same instance. Assign the output of each MIDI track to a separate input MIDI channel on the Soft Synth.

Figure 14.1. The Inspector MIDI tab

To see how this works, let's configure a multitimbral Soft Synth, using TTS-1. For this example, I will set up the Soft Synth to play piano, bass, pad, and drums from a single instance of the TTS-1 Soft Synth.

1. From the Browser Synth tab, click the Insert Synth button and select Cakewalk TTS-1 from the list. On the Insert Soft Synth Options dialog box, choose Simple instrument track to load the TTS-1 and create an instance of TTS-1 in the Synth Rack (Figure 14.2).

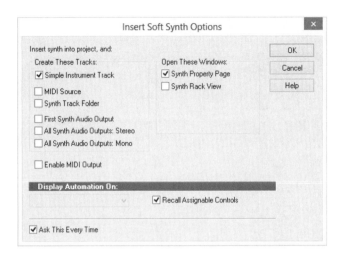

Figure 14.2. Insert Soft Synth options to add TTS-1

2. Play a few notes on your MIDI keyboard controller and you should hear sound. The newly created instrument track will play the sound assigned to channel 1 of the TTS-1. By default, this is the piano sound, which you can change by clicking the sound name and browsing other available sounds. I selected one of the other piano sounds for this example (Figure 14.3).

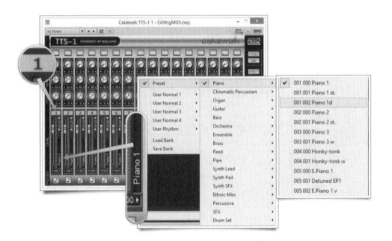

Figure 14.3. TTS-1 channel 1

3. Next, create three new MIDI tracks by right-clicking in the Track pane and selecting Insert MIDI Track for each one (Figure 14.4).
4. Name the tracks to reflect the sound they will play. The original instrument track will be piano and the three MIDI tracks will be bass, pad, and drums. Assign these sounds to channels 2, 3, and 10. Choose the appropriate presets on TTS-1 for. In adherence with general MIDI convention, I assigned the drum kit to channel 10 (Figure 14.5).

Figure 14.4. Adding the MIDI tracks

Figure 14.5. Tracks and names

5. Set the MIDI tracks output to the Cakewalk TTS-1 instance. Then, select the correct channel to match the TTS-1 channel for the correct sound—channel 2 for bass, 3 for pad, and 10 for drums. This routes MIDI note playback from each track to the correct channel on TTS-1. You can do this in the track strip, but I prefer to use the Inspector pane for these settings, as shown in Fig. 14.6.

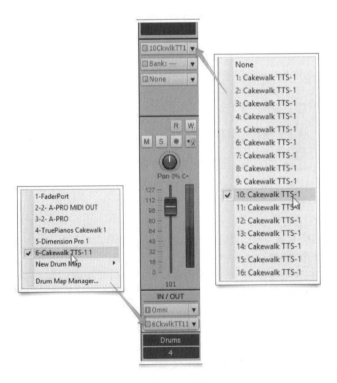

Figure 14.6. Setting MIDI track output to a TTS-1 input channel.

Although these setups are a bit tricky to understand at first, they are not that hard to configure or work with after a small amount of practice. Notice that despite there being four tracks involved in this setup, all the sound emits from the Soft Synth on the original instrument track.

> **Tip:** It's useful to create a track template for this setup, so the next time you need to use the configuration, you can right-click in the Track pane, select Insert from Track Template, and choose your saved setup. This makes it easy to recall frequently used setups; it will magically re-create the entire setup with the Soft Synth, tracks, names, and routings! To create a track template, select the appropriate tracks by dragging your mouse over the track numbers. Next, right-click one of the tracks and select "Save as Track Template."

Using Multioutput Soft Synths

Drum instruments, Such as Cakewalk Session Drummer and Toontrack EZdrummer, are the most common examples of multioutput Soft Synths. You can set up one instance of the Soft Synth, along with several stereo instrument tracks, allowing you to route kick, snares, toms, and so on, as separate Console view channels. A single MIDI track is used as source for the actual drum part MIDI performance. This setup is tedious to do piece by piece, but SONAR can do most of it automatically if you know the correct settings to use when inserting the Soft Synth.

In this example, I use Session Drummer, but the approach is similar for EZdrummer or any other comparable drum kit Soft Synth. The goal here is to configure Session Drummer with separate output channels for kick, snare, hi-hat, toms, and overheads. The drum performance will all be contained on a single MIDI track (called a source track in this situation). I will also show you how to create a track folder to hold the entire setup and save it as a track template. Here are the steps:

1. From the Browser Synth tab, click the Insert Synth button. Set up the options in the Insert Soft Synth Options, as shown in Fig. 14.7. It is important to select MIDI Source, Synth Track Folder, and All Synth Audio Outputs: Stereo. Click OK and SONAR will create twelve audio tracks and a MIDI track, conveniently organized into a track folder. The audio tracks work like stereo audio outputs from the Session Drummer mixer to the SONAR Console view mixer.

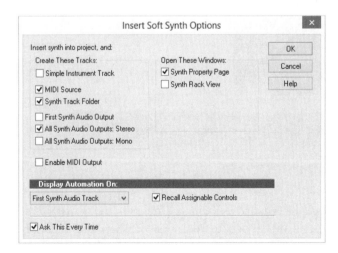

Figure 14.7. Insert Soft Synth options for Session Drummer

2. With all the tracks created, go through and name them how you intend use them. In this example, I will name them in the tradition of a conventional drum kit: Kick, Snare, HH (hi-hat), Toms, and OH (overheads). Name the track folder and the source track appropriately as shown in Fig. 14.8. The source track will hold your actual drum beat MIDI clips. Because I don't need all twelve outputs, I just delete the extra tracks. I've included sequential numbers in the track names to help in the next step.

Figure 14.8. All the tracks are named

3. Open the mixer in the Session Drummer window. Next, assign each drum to the correct output using the list at the bottom of each channel as shown in Fig. 14.9. They are numbered in the order they appear in the track folder, which is why it's smart to include the track order number when naming the tracks. Note that I assigned all toms to the Toms 4 track and all cymbals to the OH 5 track.

Figure 14.9. Assigning the Session Drummer outputs to tracks

Now you are ready to program, record, and build your drum part, using MIDI clips on the source track. All the drums appear separated in Console view and are ready for mixing—it's just like a working with a real multitrack recording. For some great drum sounds, try loading the Steven Slate OldZepKit or the Sonic Reality Motown. Find these, and other excellent kits, in the acoustic section of the Session Drummer Program Browser.

Figure 14.10. Session Drummer acoustic kits

Tip: Save this setup as a Track Template by selecting all the tracks, right-clicking, and choosing Save As Track Template. It will save an immense amount of effort the next time you want to use the same setup.

The Included Soft Synths

SONAR Producer includes lots of Soft Synths that are useful for all styles of music. Similar to the bundled effects, there is range of technology here, some of which is included for compatibility. I have sorted these into categories to guide you (and myself) as we explore this huge sound library.

Essential Instruments

I come back to these five SONAR Soft Synths time and again during my songwriting projects:

Dimension Pro. Dimension is a great sounding sample-based instrument for bread-and-butter sounds. The standard sounds are excellent and Cakewalk offers a nice range of add-ons that extend its usefulness.

Figure 14.11. Cakewalk Dimension Pro

z3ta+. Pronounced "ZAY ta plus," this is a powerhouse synth with a wide range of analog-inspired sounds. It is a great tool for synth bass, leads, pads, and killer FX sweeps. It also has a great arpeggiator and deep sound design tools, in addition to an eclectic collection of presets. This one is great fun to experiment with.

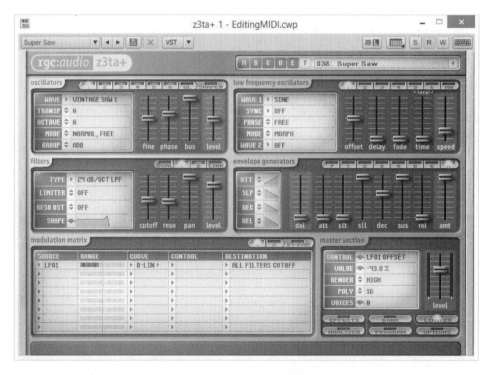

Figure 14.12. z3ta+

TruePianos Cakewalk. TruePianos was first added to SONAR in 2008 and is a light version of the full TruePianos offered by 4Front Technologies. I find it to be an easy way to get a nice piano going for songwriting. TruePianos sounds excellent when mixed with a full band and is easy to insert and use.

Figure 14.13. TruePianos Cakewalk

Rapture. Rapture is another tool for sound design and lends itself to a broad range of electronic music. Sounds are based on six elements and can be a mix of different synthesis methods. Combined with stepped filters and a range of effects, it pairs up well with z3ta+ to create EDM or ambient alien soundscapes.

Figure 14.14. Rapture

Session Drummer 3. Session Drummer is a solid, sample playback drum instrument. Version 3, launched in 2009, has some excellent included kits and beats. The key to using Session Drummer is to audition the beats by using the Media tab in the SONAR Browser. Cakewalk also offers some outstanding add-on kits for Session Drummer through the Cakewalk Store.

Figure 14.15. Session Drummer 3

Useful Tools

This set of Soft Synths is a bit older, but they are still useful tools:

Cakewalk TTS-1. Earlier in the chapter, I noted that TTS-1 is great for basic instrument sounds. It is multitimbral and works well with General MIDI files, such as karaoke tracks. Even if the sounds are bit ordinary, TTS-1 is a great way to get started on a song.

Figure 14.16. Cakewalk TTS-1

Cakewalk Studio Instruments. SI-Bass Guitar, SI-Drum Kit, SI-Electric Piano, and SI-String Section are easy-to-use single-instrument-focused Soft Synths. They actually sound really good. You might find yourself using them because they are so convenient and easy. Varying combinations of these Soft Synths are included in some of Cakewalk's entry-level products, which focus on ease of use. All of the Studio Instruments include sets of MIDI patterns you can use to audition a sound or drag to a track. The SI-String Section strings UI is a bit comical, but I find the SI-Bass to come in handy from time to time.

Figure 14.17. Cakewalk Studio Instruments

32-Bit Soft Synths

At the time of writing, these four Soft Synths had not been updated to operate in 64-bit mode. I find that these Soft Synths work reliably using SONAR's BitBridge technology. While, I hesitate to use 32-bit plug-ins on new projects, these are all very useful and I hope we see 64-bit versions in the future.

Cakewalk Sound Center. This is an easy-to-use preset-based Soft Synth that includes a full range of common instrument sounds. It is built on the sound engine of Dimension and other Cakewalk instruments, which means the sounds are excellent, while the UI is simple. Sound Center is commonly included with Cakewalk's entry-level products. Some nice add-ons from Digital Sound Factory are also available from the Cakewalk Store. It would be great to see this updated to 64-bit in the future.

Figure 14.18. Cakewalk Sound Center

DropZone. DropZone was added to the SONAR bundle as a virtual sampler instrument. It comes with a few presets, but the real power is in dragging a sample from your project right into DropZone, which in turn maps it across the keyboard. You can trim and loop the sample, layer two different elements, and apply amp simulation and modulation. I like to use it for triggering kick drum samples to layer with an acoustic kick while mixing.

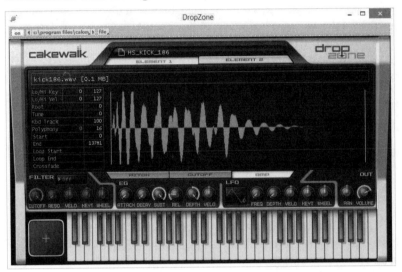

Figure 14.19. DropZone

RXP. RXP was added when SONAR 6 was released and is a great tool for working with REX files. REX is a loop format wherein the files are sliced up on the transients. The REX format is proprietary to Propellerhead Software. RXP makes it easy to map slices across a MIDI keyboard, rearrange sliced beats, and apply resonant filters. For even more fun, drag the loop out of the RXP window and drop it on an instrument track. This gives you access to a MIDI representation of the beat that will trigger the slices while keeping the timing intact.

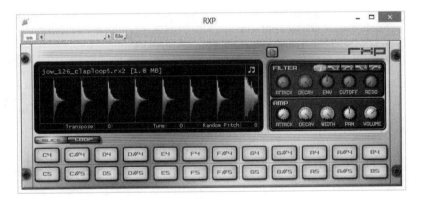

Figure 14.20. RXP

rgcAudio Square. Square is a three-oscillator virtual analog synth with all the standard, subtractive synthesis tools, chorus, and delay. With all the controls represented as knobs, it is a great tool for leads or 1980s pads and strings.

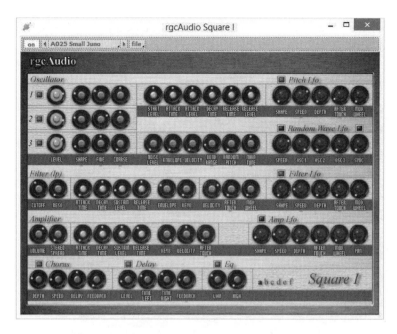

Figure 14.21. Square

Legacy Project5 Soft Synths

More than a decade ago, Cakewalk launched an interesting product named Project5. It included several Soft Synths and a lot of effects. Although Project5 (P5) was discontinued after a few years, its effects and Soft Synths have found their way into SONAR over the years. Some of these legacy instruments are from P5. There are some real gems here, particularly Cyclone.

Cyclone. Cyclone is a multioutput, pad-based drum instrument inspired by 1980s hardware units. You can assign loop samples to sixteen virtual pads, ideally mapped to a 4 x 4 pad controller. Cyclone gives you separate pitch, gain, and pan controls for each pad. You can drag sounds right from your project into Cyclone. You can also drag Groove clips and ACIDized files into Cyclone's loop editor to manipulate slices.

Figure 14.22. Cyclone

Pentagon I. Pentagon is a virtual analog synth full of knobs, great presets, and a useful amp simulator effects section. This Soft Synth is most fun when you map some knobs to a controller and automate changes. Pentagon has a formant filter that gives a vocal quality to many of the presets. Very cool.

Figure 14.23. Pentagon I

PSYN II. Yet another virtual analog synth, PSYN (pronounced like "sign") gives you another flavor of analog synthesis to go along with Square and Pentagon. It has a sixty-four-note polyphony and more controls than the others. PSYN is a good tool for synth basses and leads. While a bit more complex than Square or Pentagon, it has a big selection of presets worth listening to. Make sure to explore PSYN, Square, and Pentagon, especially if you are learning sound design for the first time. All of them will teach you the fundamentals of classic subtractive synthesis.

Figure 14.24. PSYN II

Roland GrooveSynth. This is an easy-to-use sample player loaded with classic Roland synth and drum sounds. It's useful for famous TR-808 and TR-909 drum machine sounds. These days, GrooveSynth can seem a bit redundant, and I do usually use Dimension Pro instead. However, it's light on CPU and makes a nice companion for the Step Sequencer when you get inspired to throw down classic, groove box beats.

Figure 14.25. Roland GrooveSynth

sfz SoundFont Player. Sfz is a multitimbral sound module akin to a minimalistic version of TTS-1. What's unique about sfz is its ability to load industry standard SoundFont files. Sound fonts were originally created as a way to load sounds into Creative Labs Sound Blaster PC cards. It later became a de facto standard for the exchange of sample-based instrument sounds. sfz is a useful tool for working with SoundFont-based samples.

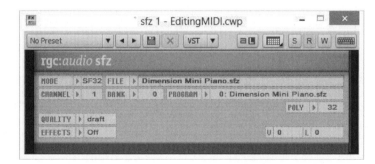

Figure 14.26. sfz SoundFont Player

With that, we delved a bit deeper into Soft Synths. Although there isn't time to cover how to use each Synth or MIDI FX and the full range of advanced tools for working with MIDI, this should be enough to get you started.

PART III: EFFECTS & MIXING

Chapter 15
CONSOLE VIEW TIPS AND TRICKS

In this chapter, we will explore types of channels in Console view, as well as learn some tips and tricks for working with channels from this view.

In a way, the Console view is redundant because you can do just about anything using the Track view and the Inspector. Seeing all your channels in parallel during mixing, however, can be comforting. Some grouping operations are best done in the Console view.

Figure 15.1. Console view

For the most part a "track" in Track view is matched to a "channel" in Console view. You can think of a track as a horizontal timeline analogous to a track on a multitrack tape machine. The channel is conceptually modeled after physical mixing desks with signal flowing from top to bottom.

Console Overview

The Console view is divided into three panes that represent channels corresponding to tracks, buses, and mains—in that order. These panes are divided by thicker lines that you can grab and resize. You can show or hide any of these from the Console view menu under Strips.

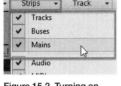

Figure 15.2. Turning on or off tracks, buses, and mains

Channels are organized into three sections that you can resize with the vertical dividing bars. Here is a brief description of the types channel sections in left-to-right order in Console view.

Figure 15.3. Console channels: tracks, buses, and mains

Tracks. This section contains channels for each track in your project. These channels either represent audio tracks or outputs from the Instruments in the Synth Rack. There are three kinds of tracks in SONAR: audio tracks, MIDI tracks, and instrument tracks.

Buses. Buses are typically used for submixes of tracks and master effects (FX). In my mixes I usually have a four or more master effects (delays and reverbs) and at least four submixes labeled Drums, Music, Vocals, and FX. By default, projects have a Master bus that serves as the stereo output for the final mix. I route all submixes to the Master.

Mains. The Mains channels represent the physical outputs from your audio interface. Typically, these will route to your monitor speakers or headphone amps.

> **Tip:** If you start up SONAR and can't seem to hear playback, check the Master bus and make sure the output is routed to the correct physical output. Sometimes this gets lost, especially if you started SONAR without your audio interface connected.

Channel Tricks

This section includes some tricks for working with channels that might not be obvious. All of these things save time if you learn how they work.

Selecting Multiple Channels. There are numerous operations that work across a selection of channels. The best way to select multiple channels is to swipe the mouse across the channel number area. Use Ctrl-click to add or subtract channels from the selection.

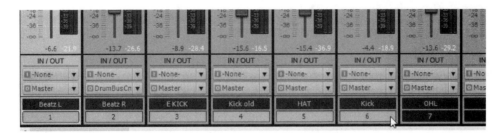

Figure 15.4. Selecting multiple tracks

Show/Hide Channels. To quickly hide the selected channels, use the shortcut Ctrl + H. Or press H to open the Track Manager, which allows you to select which tracks (and channels) to show or hide.

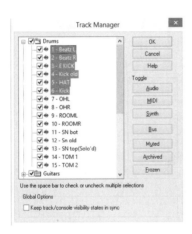

Figure 15.5. Press H for Track Manager

Reset Controls. Double-click any control to reset it to the default position. For example, double-click a pan knob to center it; double-click a volume fader to set it back to 0 dB.

Reorder Channels. To rearrange channels and buses, hold down Alt and drag left or right. A red outline will show you the where it will go when you drop it. The trick here is to drag from either side of the pan knob, as shown in Fig. 15.7.

Figure 15.6. Double-click to reset faders to 0 dB

Figure 15.7. Reordering channels

ProChannel. I cover the ProChannel in a separate chapter, but it is worth noting that clicking the ProChannel button will slide open the ProChannel to the right. If the Inspector is open to the ProChannel, it will show the one for the selected channel. However, the ProChannel cannot be opened in the Console and Inspector at the same time.

Figure 15.8. Inspector ProChannel follows channel selection

Console Metering

You can set the meter response and action separately for each channel type. We went over similar settings in the chapter covering Track view and recording. The settings for all the various meters are available under Options > Meters.

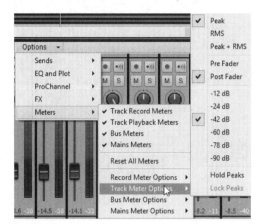

Figure 15.9. Setting the Meter options

I set the Record meters to –24 dB, Peak. I set the track, bus, and mains meters to the default 42 dB, Peak, and Post Fader, respectively. For the bus meters, I am more interested in the average, which I set to –42 dB, Peak + RMS. Note: You can quickly change the meter resolution for individual channels by right-clicking on any channel meter.

Quick Grouping

The Quick Group feature is a really nice workflow enhancement tool found in SONAR. Although not something easily discoverable, it is certainly a tool you will use once you figure it out. Quick Grouping allows you to set the same control across several channels at once, usually by adding the Ctrl key as a modifier.

Here are the examples:

Quick Group by Type

Normally, if you grab and move the volume fader, you adjust just that one thing. However, if you hold Ctrl while moving it, all faders for that type of channel move proportionally. For example, hold Ctrl and adjust the fader on one audio track, and all other audio tracks will be adjusted along with it. This works for other channel controls as well, such as the pan knob or solo button.

Quick Group by Selection

To change the corresponding setting for all the other selected channels, highlight the channel numbers, then hold Ctrl as you adjust a setting. In this scenario, the channels don't even need to be the same type. This is a great way to bring down all faders when the mix is getting too hot.

Figure 15.10. Quick Group selection

Quick Group Solo/Mute

You can extend this to the Solo button. Make a selection of channels and hit Solo on a track to toggle the on/off state on all channels. This allows you to essentially reverse the solo setting on for all channels in the group.

Quick Group ProChannel Tricks

Quick Group techniques extend to the ProChannel and make it much easier to work with more than one channel at a time. This is really helpful when setting stereo tracks left and right to match, for example. I cover the ProChannel in detail in the next chapter, but keep these in tricks in mind!

ProChannel Settings

Group a few channels, then hold down Ctrl and trying opening the ProChannel for one of them. Notice that they all open. If I want to adjust a control to make it the same on the left and the right channel of a pair of channels, all I have to do is hold down Ctrl. This works for loading ProChannel presets as well.

Figure 15.11. ProChannel Quick Group QuadCurve example

Inserting ProChannel Modules

This is really powerful when setting up a project. Select a few channels, hold down Ctrl, and right-click to insert a module. This will instantly insert the same module in all the selected channels. You can also apply this to deleting: simply hold down Ctrl and delete a module to delete it from all selected channels.

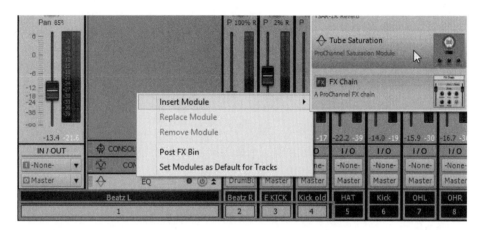

Figure 15.12. Inserting ProChannel module to several tracks, using Quick Group

Activating ProChannel Modules

As you can guess by now, holding down Ctrl as you activate a module will activate it across all selected channels. You can also use this for the master ProChannel On and Off buttons for grouped tracks to bypass all ProChannel effects.

That's an introduction to the Console view. Next let's move on to adding effects with the ProChannel.

Chapter 16

USING THE PROCHANNEL

The ProChannel is a configurable channel strip accessible from Console view or from the Inspector pane. When the ProChannel first debuted as a feature of SONAR X1, it offered only an EQ, a choice of two compressors, and tube saturation.

As of SONAR X2, the ProChannel has grown to become a fully configurable effects channel with numerous included, optional, and third-party modules. In this chapter, we will review the basics of using the ProChannel and explore QuadCurve EQ.

Accessing the ProChannel in the Inspector Pane

Click the tab labeled ProCh in the Inspector pane to see the ProChannel for any selected track (Figure 16.1). The ProChannel is available on audio tracks, instrument tracks, bus channels, and the Master bus. Click ProCh again to hide the ProChannel.

As you select different tracks in your project, the Inspector pane ProChannel will switch instantly to the selected track. This is an efficient way to work in Track view, as you don't have to constantly switch back and forth to Console view while mixing.

Accessing the ProChannel from Console View

Click the small arrow to the right of the word "ProChannel" on any channel. The ProChannel opens to the right of the other channel controls. The arrow acts as an Expand/Collapse button for the ProChannel. In Console view, you can open as many ProChannel views as you want.

Figure 16.1. The ProChannel in the Inspector pane

Figure 16.2. Click to open ProChannel in Console view

Tip: To open the ProChannel for several channels at once, select the channels and hold down Ctrl as you click the Expand/Collapse button.

ProChannel Small View

Audio, instrument, and bus channels have a ProChannel small view that contains a mini EQ Graph and a few other important options (Figure 16.3).

Here is a rundown of what these controls do:

Load/Save Presets. Use this area to save or load ProChannel presets. To apply a preset to several channels at once, select the channels, then hold down Ctrl as you load a preset (Figure 16.4).

Figure 16.3. The ProChannel small view on a channel

Post. Enables the Post button to move the entire ProChannel after the FX bin. I find this useful for adding an extra EQ to do bass roll-offs with an Insert plug-in, before going into the ProChannel. With Post turned off, ProChannel processing occurs before the FX bin (Figure 16.5).

Global Input Meter. The Global Input Meter glows when the ProChannel is processing audio—the hotter the signal, the redder it gets (Figure 16.6).

ProChannel On/Off. This button turns the entire ProChannel on and off (Figure 16.7).

Figure 16.4. Load and save ProChannel presets

Figure 16.5. ProChannel Post button

Small EQ Graph. This is a mini version of the QuadCurve EQ. Not only can you see the curve, but you can also adjust it in the small EQ Graph by dragging up and down, or left and right, within each of the four bands. Click directly on a frequency node to enable or disable a band (Figure 16.8).

Figure 16.6. ProChannel Input Meter

Figure 16.7. ProChannel on/off

EQ Plot Resolution. Right-click on the small EQ Graph to set the plot resolution. This sets the maximum vertical scale for the EQ Graph in the full ProChannel. This setting is a bit hard to discover but is very useful.

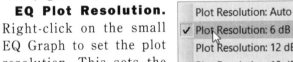

Figure 16.9. Setting the EQ Plot Resolution

Figure 16.8. ProChannel small EQ Graph

Tip: Try setting the Plot Resolution to 6 dB to help avoid over equalizing tracks. In this mode, the EQ Graph window maxes out at 6 dB—a nice visual cue indicating enough boost!

Working with ProChannel Modules

You can easily insert, remove, replace, and reorder ProChannel modules by using the right-click menu and drag-and-drop. You can also manage ProChannel presets. Here are the details:

Inserting a ProChannel Module.

Right-click on the header of any existing module or on some blank space on the ProChannel and select Insert Module, then select a module from the list (Figure 16.10). The list contains all modules available on your system. If the module shows up in the wrong place in the ProChannel, just drag it by the header to correct spot.

Figure 16.10. Adding a ProChannel module

Removing/Replacing a ProChannel Module

To remove a module, simply right-click its header and select Remove Module from the menu. You can also replace modules from the same right-click menu. Note: The QuadCurve EQ is always present and cannot be removed.

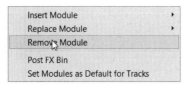

Changing the Order of Modules

To reorder ProChannel modules, drag the module you want moved by its header. Because signal flows from top to bottom, the order can have a big impact on the sound.

Figure 16.11. Removing or replacing a ProChannel module

Creating a Default ProChannel Preset

It is easy to set a default ProChannel configuration within your project:

1. On any channel, insert your favorite modules and order them to your preference. I like to use PC76 Compressor > QuadCurve EQ > Console Emulator as my standard setup.
2. Dial in any initial settings you want to use as a starting point.
3. Right-click on any module header or on some blank space and select Set Modules as Default for Tracks.

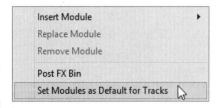

Now, whenever you create a new channel in the project, your default ProChannel will load automatically. If you want to use this same setup for future projects, save it as a preset or save the entire project as a template.

Figure 16.12. Creating a default ProChannel setup

QuadCurve Equalizer

When you open the ProChannel, one module is always there—the QuadCurve Equalizer (QuadCurve EQ). In this section, you will learn the controls of this incredibly important, ever-present module.

The QuadCurve EQ is a great general-purpose equalizer inspired by classic SSL (Solid State Logic) consoles. SSL manufactures high-end pro-studio consoles. The SSL 4000 analog mixing consoles from the 1980s and '90s are legendary for their sound and helped mix countless hit records. The controls and sound of the QuadCurve EQ are similar to those of an SSL 4000 channel. Because of the four distinct modes, you get even more flexibility than you did with the original.

Figure 16.13. The QuadCurve Equalizer module

EQ Modes

Figure 16.14. QuadCurve EQ modes

At the top of the QuadCurve EQ, you can select from four different EQ modes. Any of these modes can be used for channel or bus EQ.

Each mode imparts its own unique flavor. Here is a description of each mode:

E-Type. There were earlier SSL 4000s, but the E series was the first widely successful SSL. It is still the standard by which all modern pro consoles are measured. If you want to mix with the same EQ curves as these legendary consoles, then choose the E-Type on your channels. The E-Type bass shelf also features a low-midrange dip that is flattering to kicks, basses, and the drum bus.

G-Type. The G-Type EQ mode is modeled after the SSL 4000 G series consoles—the successor to the E-Type. This mode features a revised curve on the peaking EQs. The EQ band narrows as you increase the Level, making it easier to sweep boosts when searching for key frequencies and to reduce the Level without fiddling as much with the Q control. The low shelf is more accurate, but it doesn't have the pronounced low-midrange

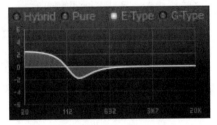

Figure 16.15. QuadCurve EQ E-Type bass boost

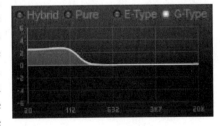

Figure 16.16. QuadCurve EQ G-Type bass boost

dip of the E-Type. The shelf EQs feature a slight rise near the cutoff frequency that enhances the perception of frequency boosts, without adding as much energy.

Hybrid. Hybrid mode works as an additional enhancement to the G-Type. It is not modeled after a specific SSL desk. The width of the peaking EQs is different for boosts and cuts at the same frequency. If you increase the Level control, boosts have a broader width; if you decrease the Level control, cuts are much narrower (Figure 16.17). This is how engineers use EQ when mixing—broader boosts for musical enhancement or making tighter cuts to pull out annoying frequencies or ringing. This is reminiscent of the ubiquitous Waves Renaissance EQ plug-in that has been a staple of pro mixers for years.

Pure Mode. Pure mode is a modern, transparent EQ that works great on the Master bus or channel EQ for acoustic instruments. Peaking EQs offer broad boosts or cuts that narrow at extreme Level settings. Shelf boosts in Pure mode have a pronounced peak at the cutoff frequency, making the EQ effect more apparent (Figure 16.18). While the behavior and curves are a bit complex, it is a simple, effective general-purpose EQ in operation.

Figure 16.17. Hybrid mode asymmetrical boost/cut

Working with QuadCurve EQ Controls and EQ Graph

Most QuadCurve EQ settings can be done by manipulating frequency nodes within the EQ plot or by using the knobs, buttons, and switches. The QuadCurve EQ has four bands, each of which has controls for Freq, Q, and Level.

Enabling/Disabling Bands. Use the buttons Low, Lo Mid, Hi Mid, and High to enable or disable the corresponding frequency bands as shown in Fig. 16.19. Alternatively, click any of the frequency nodes in the EQ Graph to disable or enable the bands.

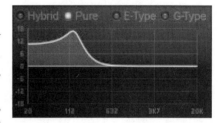

Figure 16.18. QuadCurve EQ Pure Mode bass boost

Setting the Level of Boost or Cut. Click the Level knob and drag up or down to set the Level of boost or cut. You can also drag the node for the band up or down in the EQ Plot. For finer control, hold down Shift as you drag.

Figure 16.19. Enable/disable frequency bands

Setting Frequency and Q. To set the center or crossover frequency of any EQ band, click on the Freq knob and drag up or down. Use the Q knob to set the width of the filter. You can also drag the corresponding node left or right in the EQ plot to set the frequency graphically. To set Q graphically, hold down Alt as you drag the node up and down. Again, for finer control, hold down Shift.

Setting Low/Hi Filter Type. The Low and Hi bands both have options for shelf or peak curves, which you can select with the dedicated switches as shown in Fig. 16.20.

Setting Values Directly. To set any of QuadCurve EQ values directly, double-click the numeric label and enter a number.

Figure 16.20. Selecting shelf or peak for Low and Hi bands

Figure 16.21. Setting values directly

Working with High-Pass and Low-Pass Filters

The lower section of the QuadCurve EQ has controls for High-Pass (HP) and Low-Pass (LP) filters. These filters are simple and effective. Enable or disable the filters with the HP and LP buttons. Adjust the filter frequency with the FREQ knobs. Adjust the slope of the filter with the SLOPE knobs. Slope can be adjusted from a very mild 6 dB per octave to a very steep 48 dB per octave. You can see the effect of the settings on the EQ Graph.

Figure 16.22. High-Pass and Low-Pass filters

I find the High-Pass and Low-Pass filters to be the most used aspects of the QuadCurve EQ—or of any other equalizer, for that matter. Almost every channel in a mix gets some level of high-pass filtering.

> **Tip:** If you are just using the lower section of the QuadCurve EQ, show it in a compact view (Figure 16.23). From the Console view menu, find the setting under Options > ProChannel > Compact EQ Module. In the Inspector, find the setting from the Display menu at the bottom, under Module Options > ProChannel > Compact EQ Module. The settings are global for all channels. Because you can still set the controls graphically, you don't give up any functionality. I personally use the compact view in Console view and the full view in the Inspector pane.

Figure 16.23. Compact EQ module

Working with Gloss

The Gloss button activates a subtle high-frequency lift that adds some polish to the high end. This works great to enhance cymbals, hi-hats, tambourines, or even full mixes. Simply turn it on or off by using the Gloss button.

Figure 16.24. The Gloss button

Those are the basics for using the ProChannel. In the next chapter, we will cover all of the available ProChannel modules that you can use to build your own custom console.

Chapter 17
PROCHANNEL MODULES

The SONAR ProChannel has grown to include most of the effects needed for a mix. In this chapter, I will review every module available at the time of this writing. This should help you identify which modules you need to create the perfect custom channel for your mixes.

Included ProChannel Modules

SONAR Producer ships with eight modules that define the core effects for music production. Here is a description of each of them:

Breverb 2. SONAR includes a slightly reduced version of Breverb 2 that has four different reverb algorithms—Hall, Plate, Room, and Inverse. The algorithms offer sounds similar to those of the classic Lexicon 480L. It is a fantastic reverb, with simple Dry and Wet faders and essential parameters available as knobs. Upgrade to the full version to add three more algorithms. A VST version included with SONAR has many more parameters that can be tweaked. This is a fantastic sounding reverb I use on almost every mix!

Console Emulator. New as of SONAR X2 is the Console Emulator module. It emulates the transformer input as well as subtle distortion and frequency response character of three of the most famous consoles of all time. I typically insert this first in a ProChannel setup, but others prefer to do that last.

Figure 17.1. Breverb 2 ProChannel module

Figure 17.2. Three flavors of the Console Emulator

The three options are not difficult to decode: S-Type is for SSL; N-Type, for Neve; and A-Type, for API. The Trim knob allows you to adjust the signal entering the module. Turning the drive knob up allows you to add extra overdrive distortion. Note: When used on a bus channel, Console Emulator has no Trim knob. Turn on the Tolerance switch to make each channel slightly different from the others. This emulates real consoles that vary slightly due to electronic component tolerances. Because this makes the emulation that much more accurate, I usually leave it turned on.

Console Emulator is subtle but effective when used on every channel. While experimenting, I found I prefer the S-Type, though they are all useful and subtle.

QuadCurve Equalizer. When X1 first came out, the QuadCurve EQ was originally called the GlossEQ. It has been greatly enhanced since, with a new Hybrid EQ type, color-coded knobs, and direct-edit values. It is the best SONAR equalizer to date and I detailed the operation in the previous chapter.

PC4K S-Type Bus Compressor. The name is a coded reference to the SSL 4000 bus compressor. The bus compressor is legendary for offering a unifying sound for pop and rock mixes. The compressor works great when driven hard on a drum bus or applied gently to lead vocals.

The controls on the PC4K Bus Compressor are typical of compressors: threshold, attack, release, ratio, and makeup gain. Dry/Wet knobs make it easy to use this for popular parallel compression techniques. There is also a High-Pass filter (HPF) that affects the detection circuit. It can be helpful to turn this up to reduce audible pumping in a mix with a heavy kick or bass.

When misused, a real-life SSL bus compressor causes a pumping effect on your mix. This can be used to add some energy to a song and has been used on countless hit records. To do this with the PC4K, select a fast Attack, short Release, and set Ratio to 10. Start with Dry/Wet all the way up and adjust Thresh until you get a deep gain reduction movement on the meter. Adjust Release to match the pumping to the tempo of the music.

Figure 17.3. PC4K S-Type Bus Compressor

You can also route other signals to the side chain, though we won't cover this here. If you aren't using the side chain, leave the S.Chain switch set to Off.

PC76 U-Type Compressor. This module is an emulation of the famous Universal Audio/Urei 1176LN Compressor. The 1176 has been a staple of pro studios since its debut in the late 1960s. It has a fast attack time, making it suitable for drums and flexible enough to use on almost any source. The famous all-buttons mode is represented with an infinity button on the PC76. This sets a very high ratio essentially turning the compressor into a limiter. This is a very effective effect on the drum bus if you want to make your drums loud!

The ProChannel version also offers a Mix control that makes it easy to apply parallel compression. It doesn't offer any sort of threshold control, because the Level is fixed. Adjust the Input to drive the PC76 enough to start compressing, and then balance it against the Output knob. I use the PC76 U-Type as my default channel compressor.

Figure 17.4. PC76 U-Type Compressor

ProChannel FX Chain. Insert the FX Chain module to create custom ProChannel effects. In the example shown in Fig. 17.5, I created a LoCut effect by loading a Sonitus:fx EQ and tuning it to offer six different preset low-cut (high-pass) setups. You can do this with any available combination of SONAR DX or VST effects in the ProChannel.

Figure 17.5. FX Chain module

Softube Saturation Knob. This simple and effective module adds a warm, fuzzy distortion to any channel. To change the character of the distortion, flip the switch to the Keep High or Keep Low positions. This works great on the drum bus and drum loops, or as a send effect as a type of exciter using parallel distortion.

Figure 17.6. Softube Saturation knob

Tube Saturation. The Tube Saturation is one of the three original ProChannel modules. I tend to use it less since the Console Emulator and Saturation Knob became available. It offers one or two tube stages, as well as Input, Drive, and Output knobs. Use it to add a bit of tube warmth to any sort of track. I like to use it on snares tracks to add a bit of crunch.

Figure 17.7. Tube Saturation module

Optional ProChannel Modules

Since the ProChannel became modular, Cakewalk has released several optional modules. These include more emulations of famous vintage gear and give you more tools to design the ideal channel strip.

ProChannel Concrete Limiter. The Concrete Limiter is a very effective limiter with clear metering and no latency. It is effective when you need to control peaks on any channel or bus. Although it does work on a full mix, it's not really a volume maximizer, as it doesn't have a large look-ahead buffer.

Figure 17.8. Concrete Limiter

To use the Concrete Limiter, simply lower the Ceiling knob to set maximum level you want on the Output. On the Master bus you could set it to –3 dB, then lower the Thresh control until you start to see gain reduction on the center meter. Engage the Bass switch to reduce the effect of bass energy on the limiter, which in turn decreases audible pumping in bass or kick heavy mixes.

The UI on the Concrete Limiter is clear and the metering is excellent. I hope Cakewalk follows this up with a compressor using this UI style. Highly recommended!

PC4K S-Type Expander/Gate. This is an emulation of the gate from an SSL 4000 channel strip. As an expander, it lowers volume below a threshold. Personally, I still use the Sonitus:fx Gate, because the metering is much clearer.

> **Tip:** Remember, you can drag any of the Sonitus:fx plug-ins into the FX Chain Module for use in the ProChannel.

Figure 17.9. PC4K S-Type Expander/Gate

There is no effect if the Thresh control is fully counterclockwise. Turning the Thresh clockwise, however, starts to raise the threshold. Sound below that level will be reduced based on the amount set in the Range control. That's how it works as an expander.

To make it fully gate the signal below the threshold, engage the Gate button. Release sets the amount of time the gate stays closed, which is what you need to change so the following notes aren't chopped off. Setting F.Attack to fast makes the gate kick in more quickly, which can be good or bad, depending on the source track. I usually try both positions.

PC4K S-Type Channel Compressor. This module emulates the SSL 4000 channel compressor. It rounds out the offering of SLL based modules, so if you combine it with the Expander/Gate, S-Type on the QuadCurve EQ, and S-Type on the Console Emulator, you can have a full SSL 4000 mixing experience. While it's an effective compressor, the controls are pretty clear if you have used SSL consoles in the past. Turning the Threshold knob clockwise lowers the threshold, which is the opposite of many modern compressors. Release starts at 100 ms, which is pretty long. Attack time is 33 ms, or 0.9 ms if you engage the F.Attack switch.

Figure 17.10. PC4K S-Type Channel
Compressor

If you want to use this compressor on a channel for vocals or drums, try this step by step.

1. Turn Thresh and Release controls fully counterclockwise.
2. Turn F.Attack to the On position.
3. Adjust Ratio to between 2:1 and 4:1.
4. Play back the project and turn Thresh clockwise until you see 3 to 6 dB of gain reduction on the LED meter.
5. Add make up gain with the Output knob.

Of all the available ProChannel modules, I find the PC4K S-Type Channel Compressor is the hardest with which to achieve the correct gain staging. Sometimes it helps to put another module ahead of it to boost the signal. If you are after a full SSL experience, then it's a great tool. However, it isn't my favorite ProChannel compressor, as it can be a bit tricky to dial in.

CA-2A T-Type Leveling Amplifier. This is an emulation of the classic Teletronix LA-2A. Cakewalk originally released this as the PC2A T-Type Leveling Amplifier. In early 2013, it was updated, renamed, and released as a cross-platform plug-in. Now called CA-2A, it supports ProChannel and VST on PC and AU/VST on Mac. An additional Photocell Memory option was also added, allowing you to choose between Classic and Fast Reset.

Figure 17.11. CA-2A T-Type Leveling Amplifier

The CA-2A, like the original LA-2A, does wonderful things for lead vocals, pianos, and almost any other type of track. To operate, simply adjust the Input gain against a fixed threshold, then adjust the amount of compression with the Peak Reduction knob. The Limit switch adjusts two different sets of ratios—I recommend experimenting with both settings. This is another excellent module that I highly recommend.

Softube Mix Bundle ProChannel Modules

Softube's Mix Bundle adds some outstanding modules to the ProChannel. I use all of these modules in my mixes. In addition to the ProChannel versions, the Mix Bundle includes the full VST/AU versions for PC and Mac, making it a great value. Each module has a small logo somewhat resembling a Cyclops's smile. Click the logo to check for updates or to load its PDF manual.

Note: The Softube Mix Bundle requires the use of a USB iLok dongle for copy protection.

TSAR-1R. The TSAR-1R is a fantastic but very simple algorithmic reverb. With just two sliders, it is super easy to dial a great-sounding reverb. This unit is true stereo, meaning the left and right channels are processed separately and appropriately.

> **Tip:** Try using TSAR-1R as a lead vocal slap-back echo by selecting a Predelay time just below 200 ms and using the Studio or Room setting for Time.

Figure 17.12. Softube TSAR-1R Reverb

Passive Equalizer. The Passive Equalizer is modeled after a rare Neumann PEV 930 Console Equalizer. It is a wonderful-sounding EQ, but take the control labels with a grain of salt. The controls interact, making the markings less than accurate. Regardless, it is tuned in a way that will flatter most sources, especially on the high end. This EQ also works great on overhead drums.

> **Tip:** Try setting the presence control to 0.7 kHz and boosting on your snare track. This can do wonders to fatten up an otherwise dull snare!

Figure 17.13. Softube Passive Equalizer

Active Equalizer. This EQ is modeled after a Swiss console channel EQ—the Filtek Labo mk.5. It features three parametric bands with a selection of wide and narrow filter shapes and stepped controls. It is not subtle and can add some punch to any kind of track. This EQ makes a great companion to the QuadCurve EQ.

Tip: Try putting the Active Equalizer module above any of the compressor modules and Low Cut to roll of lows before your compressor module. Follow the compressor with the QuadCurve for boosts and creative EQ. Active Equalizer makes a nice companion anytime you want two EQs on a track.

Figure 17.14. Softube Active Equalizer

Focusing Equalizer. Once you use the Softube Focusing Equalizer, you'll wonder how you ever mixed without it! Its unique design works by setting low- and high-cut filters. Adjusting the filter also adjusts the Low Boost and High Boost frequencies. This simplifies the most common way to create EQ kicks, snares, and bass guitar. It works well on all kinds of tracks, but it is simply amazing for tweaking kicks. Also highly recommended.

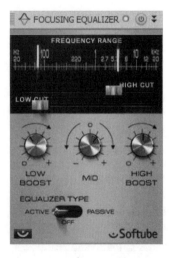

Figure 17.15. Softube Focusing Equalizer

FET Compressor. The FET compressor is another 1176-style compressor in the same vein as the PC76 U-Type Compressor. It is another very nice emulation, with its advantage being that the FET compressor has continuously variable ratio control. This helps dial in the in-between ratios, such as 1.5:1 or 2.5:1, that you can't do with a typical 1176. I actually much prefer the full version of the FET compressor, as it also has a mix control and a controls to EQ the detector circuit.

Figure 17.16. Softube FET
Compressor

As this book was just about finished, Cakewalk released the Overloud Vintage Keyboard FX ProChannel modules. These effects are modeled after classic synth effects and should offer some great new options for ProChannel mixing. I haven't gotten my hands on them yet, but I am particularly excited about the Delay effect since until now, there was no dedicated ProChannel delay. Make sure to check with Cakewalk for new modules. It's a pretty good bet that Cakewalk has since released more.

Chapter 18
USING PLUG-IN EFFECTS

I n the last two chapters, we covered using the SONAR ProChannel to add effects to your song. There is an entirely different way to add effects using the FX bin, located on audio, instrument, and bus channels of the Console view mixer. In practice, it works similarly to the ProChannel, except you don't get the organized channel strip view. Instead, each effect has its own pop-up window and unique UI.

Using the FX bin for effects is the traditional way of applying effects in SONAR—and most other DAWs, for that matter. Before the ProChannel was launched in SONAR X1, this was the only way to apply effects. This type of effect allows you to use all the included plug-ins, which I describe in the chapter after this. It also opens up the world of third-party VST plug-ins, of which hundreds are available.

The FX Bin

You will find the FX bin in the Console view, Inspector pane, or the track strip. FX bins are available on audio, instrument, and bus tracks/channels. Because SONAR is so configurable, it might be hidden. I commonly add FX during mixing in Console view. If you don't see FX bins on the channels, then make sure the FX bin option is selected under Modules > FX Bin on the Console view menu (Figure 18.1).

Add an effect easily by dragging it from the Browser and dropping onto the FX bin of any channel. To do this, open the Browser (B), click the Plug-ins tab, click the Audio FX button, and then navigate to the effect you want to use. Now drag the effect to the FX bin. In reality, you can drop it just about anywhere on a channel and it will load the effect into the FX bin. Note: If you drop an effect on a clip in Track view, it will load as a clip effect, which is probably not what you want at this point. More on that shortly.

Figure 18.1. Showing the FX Bin in Console view

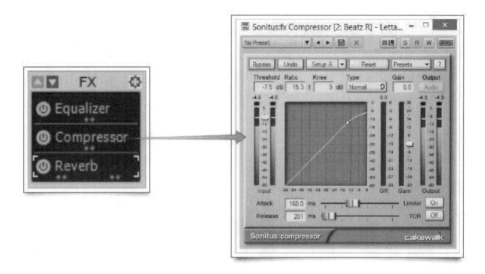

Figure 18.2. Opening a plug-in window

To open the window for a plug-in effect, double-click its name in the FX bin (Figure 18.2). From there, you can tweak the parameters during playback to suit the mix.

Working with Audio FX Plug-ins and the FX Bin

The signal flow travels from top to bottom and from one effect to the next. Let's review the details of working with the FX bin:

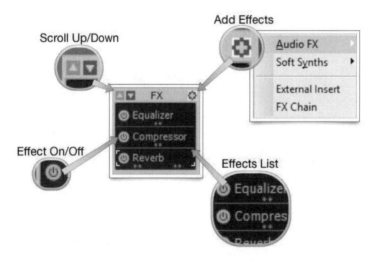

Figure 18.3. FX Bin details

Reorder Effects. To reorder effects, drag one from the list to where you want it. A red line will guide you in targeting the new position.

Delete an Effect. To delete an effect, right-click and select Delete from the drop-down menu.

Turn and Effect On/Off. Press the blue On/Off button next the effect name to turn it on or off.

Scroll Up/Down. If you have a large number of effects in an FX bin, there won't be room to see them all in the list. Use the scroll Up/Down arrows in the top left corner to see any that are hidden.

Add Effects. We just reviewed adding effects by dragging and dropping them from the Browser. To add them, you can also click the plus in the upper right corner and select Audio FX.

Other Plug-in Types and the FX Bin

When you click the Add Effects button you will notice that there are additional effects (Figure 18.3). Although there is not room in this book to cover some of the more advanced details, I summarized these options to give you a taste.

Soft Synths. Normally, you add Soft Synths to instrument tracks. However, you can also add them to the FX bin of any audio track, which allows you to create an audio track to accompany a MIDI track. This is how Soft Synths were handled before instrument tracks and is still supported for compatibility.

External Insert. This loads a special plug-in configured to route to external hardware and back, right on the track as an insert. It is a cool way to use external analog or rack processors for mixing in SONAR. You will need an interface with some extra ins and outs, and a bit of patience, to configure it.

FX Chain. The FX Chain is another special type of plug-in that allows you to load a full configuration of multiple effects, as if it were one effect. I won't get into creating them here, but you will want to explore the presets for inspiring ways to combine effects. The ProChannel has a similar FX Chain module that allows you to work with FX chains in the ProChannel as well. So much to explore!

Clip Effects

As I mentioned before, you can drag and drop an effect right onto a clip. The effect loads into the Clip Properties for that clip only. It is a great way of applying effects to just part of a track. For example, separate the last word of a phrase into its own clip, then drag a delay effect onto the clip to apply echo to just that word.

Clip effects can be tricky to work with, because you might not realize they are there. Clips with a clip effect loaded will show FX in the upper right corner.

Figure 18.4. Clip with Clip FX

Click on the word "FX" in the upper right corner to open a mini FX bin right on the clip. From there, you can open, delete, and reorder effects.

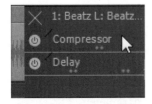

Figure 18.5. Clip FX Bin on the clip

Another way to see the clip FX is to select the clip, open the Inspector, and click the Clip properties tab. This also gives you access to an FX bin for the clip.

Figure 18.6. Clip FX Bin in the Inspector

Controls Common to all FX Plug-ins

All SONAR FX plug-ins share a common set of controls along the top of the pop-up FX window. These include preset management, automation controls, and track Solo buttons.

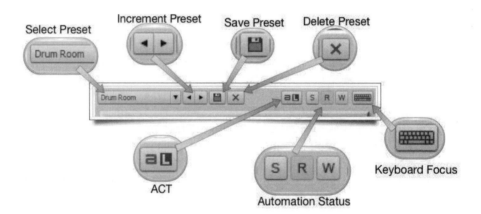

Figure 18.7. FX plug-ins common controls

Preset Controls. These controls allow you to select, save, and delete presets for use in SONAR. Third-party and included plug-ins have their own preset systems separate from this. These presets will only work in SONAR.

ACT Learn. If you have a MIDI controller configured that has physical knobs or faders, you can quickly assign an effect parameter to a hardware knob. This can be tricky, but here are the steps.

1. Enable ACT in the Act Module on the Command bar.
2. Click the ACT Learn button on the plug-in, then adjust an on-screen control in the plug-in to link it to a hardware knob.
3. Next, twist the hardware knob a bit.
4. Finally, click the ACT Learn button a second time, to remember and activate the link.

There is much more to ACT than I have space for here, but that should give you one of the most useful things to do with it.

Solo. These are convenient duplicates for the track Solo buttons. This makes it easy to solo what you are working on while you adjust effects parameters.

Automation Status. These are handy shortcuts to the automation read and write modes. If you are automating effects in plug-ins, these are incredibly useful.

Keyboard Focus. This allows the plug-in to accept typed characters when the plug-in window is open. Sometimes plug-in and SONAR key commands overlap. Keyboard focus gives the plug-in first dibs over what you type.

Those are the elements common to all effects. Let's move on to how to apply effects in your mix.

Master Effects

An "insert" effect involves adding effects to a channel's FX bin or ProChannel for audio and instrument tracks. The processing is done only for that channel. You mix the effect by using the mix control directly on the effect, including for such special effects as reverb, chorus, distortion, and delay.

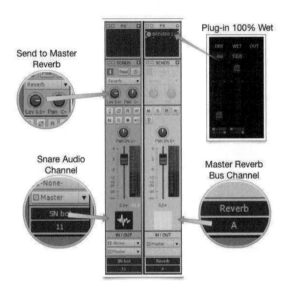

Figure 18.8. Master reverb effects bus setup

You apply a master effect, on the other hand, by using the Send knob on channels to "send" some of the signal over to the master effect's bus channel. One of the major benefits of this scheme is the ability to use the same effect for several channels— allowing you to better tie things together so as to produce a more unified sound. It also conserves CPU power, compared to loading a new instance of the effect on many channels. I usually have four or more master effects configured for a typical mix—two master delays and two master reverbs.

> **Tip:** On master effects bus channels, it is imperative to set the mix on each plug-in FX to 100 percent wet. You don't want the dry signal to pass through the effect, because that level is handled on the original channel.

It's not difficult to set up master effects; however, there are several steps: adding a bus channel; inserting the effect; then on any channel, assigning the send to the bus. There is an easier way, though. That is to use the Insert Send Assistant. Right-click the send section for any channel to which you want apply the master effect, then select Insert Send Assistant from the menu.

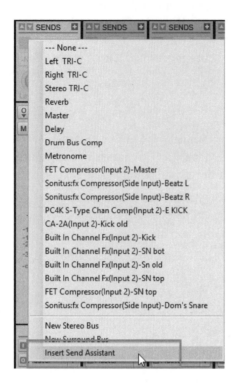

Figure 18.9. Starting the Insert Send Assistant

Next, fill out all the sections of the Insert Send Assistant form to automate the setup.

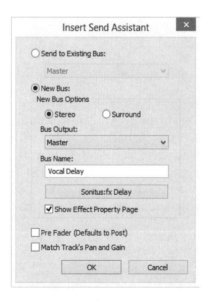

Figure 18.10. The Insert Send Assistant

Apply a master effect to an additional channel by clicking the Add button in the Send area of the channel and selecting the bus.

Figure 18.11. Routing a Send to an existing master effect

Normally, only a single Send section is shown per channel. To add another Send, use Options > Sends > Send Display 2.

Figure 18.12. Adding a second Send to channels

You now have a solid introduction into using and setting up effects, the FX bin, and master effects. In the next chapter, I will review the plug-in effects included with SONAR.

Chapter 19
THE INCLUDED EFFECTS PLUG-INS

When applying effects in SONAR, I typically lean toward ProChannel effects. It's easy to forget that SONAR Producer includes dozens of VST and DX plug-ins. Cakewalk has been continuously developing SONAR for almost twenty years. With each version, they continue to release new effects. I counted over fifty plug-ins beyond the core ProChannel modules!

Which of these effects should you use? In this chapter, we'll review these bundled effects and how they fit into the history of SONAR. I have indicated my favorite effects with the word "ESSENTIAL." I hope this helps you decide which to use in your projects. I will start by reviewing how to hide effects you don't use.

To see the installed plug-in effects, go to the Browser (B) and select the Plug-ins tab and the Audio FX button (Figure 19.1). Use the menu on the tab to select the Default All Plug-ins layout.

This is the default view of the installed effects. I have a mix of bundled and third-party effects on my system. Consider excluding the ones you don't use so as to create a better-organized list of effects. I will cover that in this chapter, but first let's take a look at the available effects.

There is a big list of effects to install or ignore when you install SONAR (Figure 19.2). If you choose the recommended installation, the SONAR installer will preselect thirty-eight of these.

Most users select "full install" or "recommended," both of which will load your system with effects, new and old. Note: The installer does not have a perfect one-to-one match with the plug-ins. Some installer options install more than one plug-in and the names are not always a exactly the same as what gets installed.

Figure 19.1 Browser all plug-ins layout

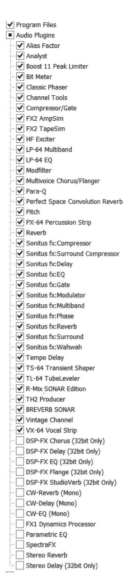

Figure 19.2 SONAR X2 effects installation choices

Excluding Unused Effects

Disable effects you don't use by navigating to Utilities > Cakewalk Plug-in Manager (Figure 19.3). Notice that the Plug-in Categories are on the left. The first two categories are for audio effects—DirectX Audio Effects (DX) and VST Audio Effects (VST).

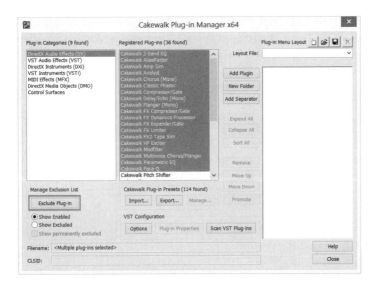

Figure 19.3. Cakewalk Plug-in Manager

Select either DirectX Audio Effects or VST Audio Effects from the Plug-in Categories list. The Registered Plug-ins list in the center shows all plug-ins of that type. To exclude a plug-in, select it in the list and click Exclude Plug-in. Restore any excluded plug-in by clicking Show Excluded, then select it from the list. Click Enable Plug-in and it will return to the Registered Plug-ins list.

I use this feature to disable both older effects and those I simply don't use.

Legacy DirectX Effects

Back in the 1990s, Cakewalk only supported the DirectX (DX) technology for effects. Today, VST has become the industry standard—though SONAR will still load and run legacy DX plug-ins. The program files for these effects have an .ax extension.

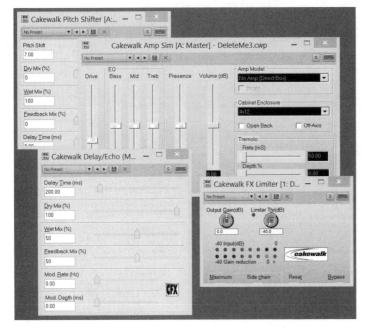

Figure 19.4. Legacy DirectX effects

Unless you want to see what effects were like back in the day, you can probably skip the AX effects during installation or exclude them with the Plug-in Manager. I did a full install on my system and found the legacy effects included all of these:

- Cakewalk 2-band EQ
- Cakewalk Amp Sim
- Cakewalk Chorus (Mono)
- Cakewalk Delay/Echo (Mono)
- Cakewalk Flanger (Mono)
- Cakewalk FX Compressor/Gate
- Cakewalk FX Dynamics Processor
- Cakewalk FX Expander/Gate
- Cakewalk FX2 Tape Sim
- Cakewalk Parametric EQ
- Cakewalk Pitch Shifter
- Cakewalk Reverb
- Cakewalk Reverb (Mono)
- Cakewalk Time/Pitch Stretch 2

P5 Half Rack Effects

Back in 2003, Cakewalk introduced a loop-based composition program called Project5 (P5). Project5 boasted a collection of "Half Rack" style effects, along with virtual instruments and other composition tools. Project5 never really took off and was discontinued, but its effects and instruments found their way into other Cakewalk products, including Guitar Tracks and Music Creator. In 2009, they were added to the SONAR 8.5 release.

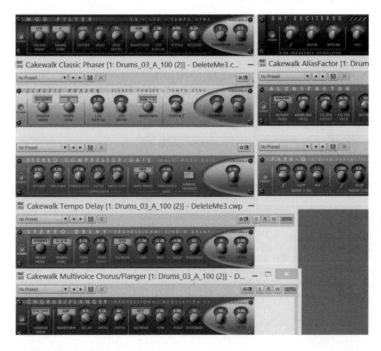

Figure 19.5. P5 Half Rack effects

The Half Rack effects cover creative, beat-synced territory, but I find them to have dated UI design, devoid of metering, as compared to modern technology. This isn't to say they aren't fun to play with, but I no longer mix with these effects and choose to exclude them on my system. The P5 effects are based on the DirectX plug-in technology rather than current VST standard.

The P5 Half Rack effects are:

- Cakewalk Alias Factor
- Cakewalk Classic Phaser
- Cakewalk Compressor/Gate
- Cakewalk HF Exciter
- Cakewalk Modfilter
- Cakewalk Multivoice Chorus/Flanger
- Cakewalk Para-Q
- Cakewalk Tempo Delay

Sonitius Effects

In 2003, Cakewalk integrated the Sonitus:fx suite of effects into SONAR 3. This superb effects suite was originally created and marketed by a company called Ultrafunk. Since then, the well-designed Sonitus effects have been essential to mixing with SONAR. The ProChannel is starting to replace these classic plug-ins, though you probably want to keep them available. The Sonitus Delay is my favorite delay plug-in of all time and I use it as a master delay in virtually every SONAR project.

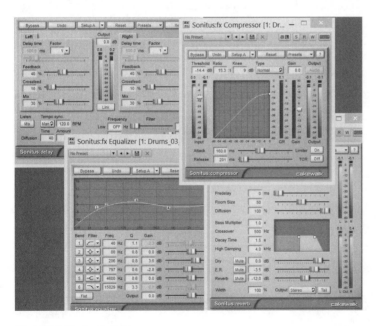

Figure 19.6. Sonitus:fx Suite

Because I currently don't do any work with surround sound, I exclude the two surround oriented Sonitus effects. Here is the full list:

- Sonitius:fx Compressor ESSENTIAL
- Sonitius:fx Delay ESSENTIAL
- Sonitius:fx Equalizer ESSENTIAL
- Sonitius:fx Gate ESSENTIAL
- Sonitius:fx Modulator
- Sonitius:fx Multiband
- Sonitius:fx Phase

- Sonitius:fx Reverb
- Sonitius:fx Surround
- Sonitius:fx SurroundComp
- Sonitius:fx Wahwah

Mastering Effects

SONAR's linear phase mastering effects were released in 2007 with SONAR 7. Later, other effects would use the same linear phase technology, with the advantage of having very little coloration or phase related side effects. The disadvantage is slightly higher latency. These effects are flexible and work very well, considering they are included with the SONAR Producer bundle. I often use the excellent third-party Izotope Ozone when I have it available as an alternative to these three tools.

LP-64 Linear Phase EQ. LP-64 EQ is a well-designed, accurate EQ plug-in. It works great on the Master bus or in complement with the QuadCurve Equalizer. It adds no color, just very clean and accurate equalization. It does use a bit more processor and adds a small amount of latency so usually it is used for mastering.

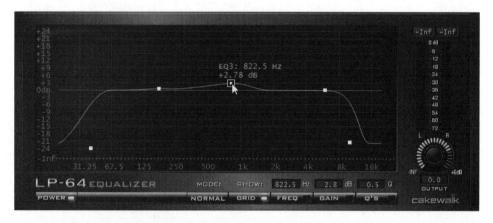

Figure 19.7. LP-64 Equalizer

Figure 19.8. LP-64 Multiband Compressor

LP-64 Multiband Compressor. This compressor has five separate compressors operating in parallel on different frequency bands. It has a nicely designed UI and works well on the drum bus, as well as for mastering and for changing the tonal balance of loops.

Boost 11 Peak Limiter. Boost 11 is designed to be a final processor for mastering and will increase the average volume of a full mix. It does work for this if used carefully. It has a nice, straightforward UI. If you don't have one of the popular third-party maximizing plug-ins (e.g., Slate FG-X, Waves L2, or Izotope Ozone) you will find Boost 11 to be a great tool—if you don't overdo it.

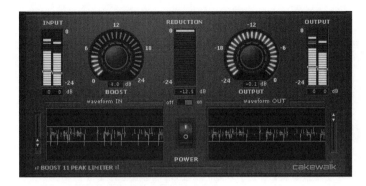

Figure 19.9. Boost 11 Peak Limiter

Channel Strips

Prior to SONAR X1, Cakewalk released three different channel strip plug-ins that provide an all-in-one solutions for track processing. I rarely use these now that the ProChannel is available. These effects do sound great, but the UIs tend to be overly complicated.

VC-64 Vintage Channel. The VC-64 was added in 2006 and sports a gate, de-esser, two compressors, and two EQs. Designed in conjunction with Kjaerhus Audio, it uses component-level modeling. At the time, it really pushed plug-in technology forward. It still sounds great, but I find the UI is so complicated that I usually pass it up for simpler, more-focused plug-ins.

Figure 19.10. VC-64 Vintage Channel

PX-64 Percussion Strip. Added to SONAR 8.5 in 2009, the PX-64 is a cool and comprehensive plug-in designed for drum tracks or the drum bus. It includes a transient shaper, compressor, expander, EQ, delay, and saturation. It's a great tool to mangle a beat or process drums or loops, though a bit complicated due to the number processing stages. It is manageable once you get the hang of it.

Figure 19.11. PX-64 Percussion Strip

VX-64 Vocal Strip. The VX-64, a multieffect optimized for vocals, also came with SONAR 8.5. It features a de-esser, compressor/expander, EQ, doubler, delay, and saturation. The UI is very similar to the PX-64 and it still holds up as great way to process vocals.

Figure 19.12. VX-64 Vocal Strip

Other Effects

TL-64 Tube Leveler. The TL-64, added to SONAR in 2008, is a saturation effect with a low-end roll-off EQ. It is based on detailed component-level modeling provided by third-party plug-in maker Studio Devil. It has many uses, particularly on the drum bus. Now that the ProChannel has numerous saturation options, the TL-64 doesn't get much use in my mixes. It is, however, an excellent tool to get realistic tube warmth on any track or bus.

Figure 19.13. TL-64 Tube Leveler

TS-64 Transient Shaper. This is a fantastic tool for shaping your kick and snare sounds. I use this plug-in on almost every SONAR mix. The Attack and Weight knobs are a much more direct way to control kicks and snares, as compared to using a compressor. ESSENTIAL.

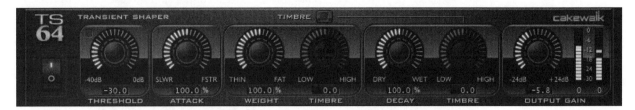

Figure 19.14. TS-64 Transient Shaper

SpectraFX. This crazy effect goes back to 2003 and descended from Plasma FXPad(2001). It is not installed by default, but is still worth a listen if only for its crazy beat-synced sweeps and filters.

Figure 19.15. SpectraFX

Perfect Space Reverb. Perfect Space debuted with SONAR 5 and was developed in cooperation with the Russian plug-in maker Voxengo. To date, Perfect Space hasn't made the jump to 64-bit. It is a great sounding convolution-style reverb that uses natural impulse responses to model real spaces. I have used it on many mixes as a master reverb. These days, I use the Softube TSAR-1R Reverb instead, because it is 64-bit and has a convenient ProChannel module version. I also have other excellent 64-bit third-party convolution reverbs that substitute nicely for Perfect Space.

Figure 19.16. Perfect Space Reverb

External Insert. You use External Insert like any other plug-in. It simply gives you tools to route out to and back from your physical hardware effects. It is a great way to patch in your vintage compressors, EQs, and stomp boxes. You will need an audio interface with extra inputs and outputs, as well as a few patch cables, to make this work.

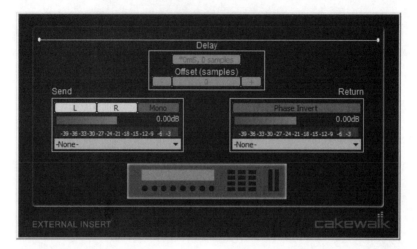

Figure 19.17. External insert

Channel Tools. Channel Tools is a Swiss Army knife plug-in used to control the stereo image and to add simple delays. I use it in some capacity on virtually every SONAR mix. ESSENTIAL.

Figure 19.18. Channel tools

New Effects in SONAR X2

R-Mix Cakewalk. R-Mix Cakewalk is a simplified version of Roland's R-Mix software. The Cakewalk version works as a VST plug-in, rather than a stand-alone program. This makes it easy to use on any track in your project. In short, it represents harmonic content on the Harmonic Placement Window. It can be used to remove parts, to EQ, or to reduce noise within a mix or part. It is an interesting effect and well worth exploring.

The Included Effects Plug-ins

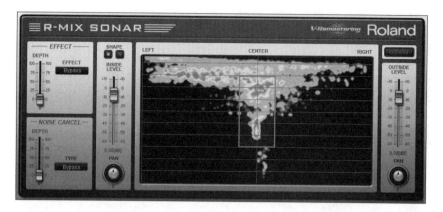

Figure 19.19. R-Mix Cakewalk

Breverb SONAR. The excellent effect from Overloud is a superb algorithm reverb. Even better, it includes a ProChannel Version. Breverb SONAR has quickly become my go-to reverb effect when using SONAR. ESSENTIAL.

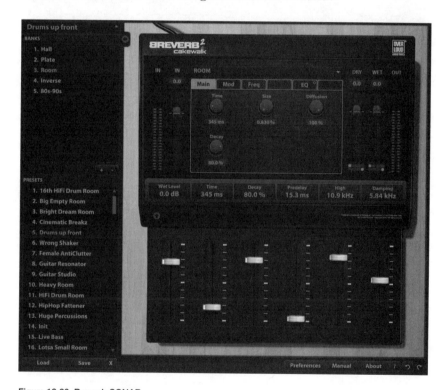

Figure 19.20. Breverb SONAR

Overloud TH2 Producer. This is a reduced version of Overloud TH2 and offers simulations of full guitar amp setups. You get amps from Randall and THD, along with other generic amps and effects and cabinets. If you like TH2, you can upgrade to the full version for a reduced price. The UI takes a bit to learn, but it is nice addition to SONAR.

Figure 19.21. Overloud TH2 Producer

Tip: Click Search to get to the preset page in TH2. It took me a while to discover this when I first started using TH2.

Chapter 20
MIXING DOWN AND EXPORTING

In this chapter, you will learn how to create a final mix. I will also show you how to share music created in SONAR by creating a .wav file, an MP3 file, a digital release using SoundCloud, or a CD disc.

Prepare the Final Mix

Using the tools we have covered in the book, adjust the levels and effects until your song sounds amazing. Check the included DVD for video examples of mixing a song.

Before you export or publish any of the music, make sure none of your levels are overloading or going into the red. I usually use Console view for this and also insert the Concrete Limiter on the Master channel. These days, I try to keep peaks at least 3 db below full scale. Full scale is the top of the meter. To assist me, I set the Concrete Limiter to –3 db and adjust all the track levels to a point where I get little to no gain reduction.

It also works well to apply a bit of the PC4K Bus Compressor before the Limiter. The PC4K is based on the famous SSL 4000 studio consoles, and the bus compressor is key to why they sound so good. If I use any EQ on the Master bus, I choose the Pure setting on QuadEQ. I really don't like to apply EQ at this phase, but if I do, I use it sparingly and with the Pure setting.

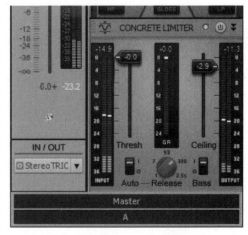

Figure 20.1. Concrete Limiter on the Master bus

Figure 20.2. PC4K bus compressor
on the Master bus

Exporting to a .wav File

Now it's time to get a song mixed down to a final product. First, let's look at exporting it as a .wav file. The process is actually very simple. Navigate to File > Export > Audio from SONAR's main menu. This opens the Export Audio dialog box.

Figure 20.3. Export Audio dialog box

Navigate to where you want to create the file and enter a filename. The settings shown in Fig. 20.3 are typical for mixing down to a 16-bit file. If you are sending out the files for professional mastering, then you probably want to set the Sample Rate and Bit Depth properties to match your current project settings and let the mastering engineer adapt those for a CD.

When the settings are all in place, click Export and wait for SONAR to process the mix and create the file. When the process is complete, find it on your system and open it in Windows Media Player to test it.

> **Tip:** I like to save a location preset in the Browser for the folder to which I export mixes. This makes it easy to find them after the export is finished. To do this, go to the Browser Media tab, navigate to your mixes folder, and then click the Save Content Location button.

Figure 20.4. SONAR mixes location in the Browser

Burning a CD

SONAR includes the Audio CD Burner utility used to create test and master CDs of your album. You can send this to an engineer to have a CD made, but most often this is used to create CDs to play in your car or to give to the band. To burn a CD, navigate to Utilities > Burn Audio CD under the main menu.

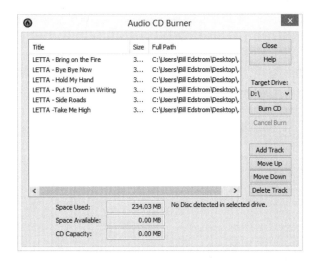

Figure 20.5. Audio CD Burner dialog box

In the Audio CD Burner, use the Add Track button to add all your mixed songs to a CD. You can do this all at once by holding Shift and selecting the files. Use the Move Up and Move Down buttons to order the songs, and then insert a blank CD and click Burn CD. In a few minutes, you will have a CD ready to play.

Exporting to MP3

Exporting to an MP3 file works similarly to exporting to a .wav file. The key difference is to choose MP3 as the file type in the Export Audio dialog box. SONAR includes a thirty-day trial version of the Cakewalk MP3 Encoder, but after that you won't be able to export an MP3 without buying a license for the encoder. It's a low-cost option and very convenient if you want to create MP3 files. You only need to buy it once for it to work with the current and all future releases of SONAR.

Digital Release to SoundCloud

SoundCloud is a fantastic music-sharing site that makes it easy to upload your music online, share it with others, embed it on your blog, post it on Twitter, and even share it on Facebook. To release a song to SoundCloud, navigate to Utilities > Share with SoundCloud under the main menu. This opens the Connect with SoundCloud window.

Figure 20.6. Connect With SoundCloud

If you're not yet a member of SoundCloud, click the link to go to the website and sign up. Once you have your password, fill in your credentials and click Allow to connect. This opens the SoundCloud form where you enter all the upload info.

Figure 20.7. Cakewalk SoundCloud form

Complete the form, including the song title, metadata, and any artwork. You can also automatically post to Twitter and Facebook, though to do so you must configure those options for your account at SoundCloud.com. Lastly, click Share and the song will start uploading. Depending on the speed of your Internet connection, this might take some time. You can upload either MP3 or .wav files to SoundCloud. Use .wav files for the best sound quality. However, because MP3 files are typically smaller and upload much faster, they are better suited to slower connections.

Figure 20.8. SoundCloud upload progress

After the upload, click the SoundCloud link to go directly to SoundCloud. At first, you will see a message indicating that SoundCloud is preparing the track for the SoundCloud playback. After a few minutes, it will be ready to go. From the

SoundCloud website, you can play the track; add comments to different sections; post it on Facebook, Twitter, or Tumblr; e-mail it; or just grab its link and embed it on any website.

Click on Stream to scroll through, play, or share any of the tracks uploaded from SONAR.

Figure 20.9. The song in SoundCloud

You should now have a good understanding of how to publish your music by exporting it to a .wav file or an MP3 file, or by burning it to a CD or publishing it on SoundCloud.

Chapter 21
ACTIVE CONTROLLER TECHNOLOGY

Active Controller Setup (ACT) allows deep integration between SONAR and MIDI controllers that support the ACT protocol. By and large, these are Roland and Cakewalk branded controllers. ACT is an advanced topic, but we'll briefly introduce ACT by giving you an example of how to configure it with a Roland A-PRO keyboard. ACT unlocks the knobs, faders, and transport controls on the A-PRO, giving you a hands-on experience with SONAR. After completing the simple steps to set up ACT, you can start taking advantage of this often-overlooked capability. ACT works similarly to the VS-700 controllers, which offer an even advanced hands-on experience. Although we won't review the VS-700 in this book, the setup is very similar to what I outline here.

Configuring SONAR to Use ACT

In Chapter 4, I explained how to configure a MIDI keyboard controller by using the Roland A-500PRO. Before the ACT feature will work properly, verify that all the MIDI in and out devices have been selected for the unit on the Devices page, found in the Preferences dialog box. The input A-Pro 2 is used specifically for the control knobs, faders, and transport controls on the A-500Pro. Note I have renamed the A-Pro 2 input to A-Pro Control.

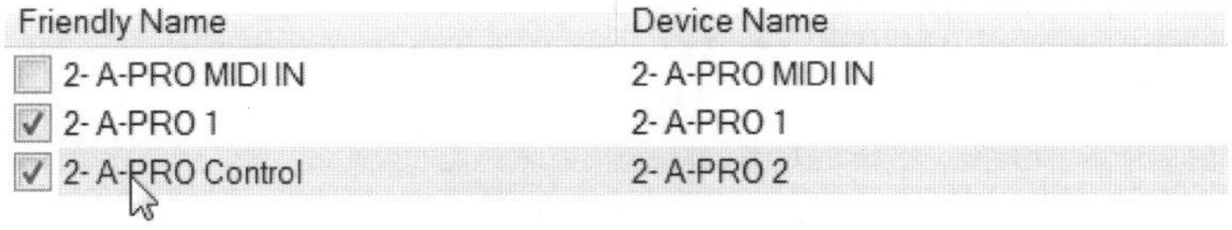

Friendly Name	Device Name
☐ 2- A-PRO MIDI IN	2- A-PRO MIDI IN
☑ 2- A-PRO 1	2- A-PRO 1
☑ 2- A-PRO Control	2- A-PRO 2

Figure 21.1. MIDI input devices in the Preferences dialog box

Once you have verified the device settings, move on to the Control Surfaces page in Preferences. Set up the parameters as shown in Fig. 21.2. Pay particular attention to the InPort setting, because if not set to the correct device for the control surface functions, ACT won't work.

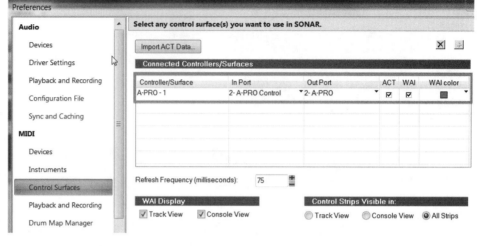

Figure 21.2. Control Surfaces settings in the Preferences dialog box

Where Am I?

In the setup, you will notice that WAI is selected in addition to ACT. WAI stands for "Where Am I?" With WAI enabled, SONAR presents a color stripe along the edge of channels and tracks controlled by the A-Pro faders (Figure 21.3). There are only eight faders on this particular keyboard, so it can only control eight at a time. The eight being controlled will show up flagged with the color you pick in this setup. Drag the WAI indicator to control a different set of eight, if you like.

There is an option to enable WAI Display for Track view, Console view, or both. If you are just getting started with SONAR and don't understand what this means, then just copy the setup. Review this again after you get more familiar with the Track view and Console view.

Figure 21.3. WAI indicator in Track view

Using ACT to Control SONAR Functions

Once you apply the setup options, your keyboard should automatically enter ACT mode. If not, press the ACT button or try resetting the keyboard. You will also want to add the ACT module to the Command Bar.

The ACT Command Bar module allows you quick access to the Controller/Surface Properties. When you press the Properties button, a Properties window will appear, customized to your specific controller. For the Roland A-Pro series of keyboards, it will look like the image in Fig. 21.5.

Figure 21.4. The ACT Command Bar module

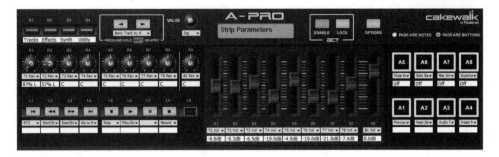

Figure 21.5. ACT controller/surface properties for the Roland A-Pro keyboards

This virtual representation of the A-Pro control section gives a complete guide to how the knobs, faders, buttons, and transport controls are mapped. While this might seem like an advanced feature, it is easy to set up with a compatible keyboard. Setting it up gives you some real advantages and is an excellent illustration of the power in SONAR.

Closing Thoughts

That brings us to the end of the book. Enjoy making music with SONAR. Good luck!

APPENDIX: ABOUT THE DVD-ROM

The DVD-ROM included with this book contains video tutorials designed to help you understand SONAR features and techniques discussed in *The Power in Cakewalk SONAR*. The videos allow you hear and see the software in action and help bring the concepts to life.

Figure A-1. Letta album

Special thanks to singer/songwriter Letta for giving me permission to use her song "Hold My Hand" for examples in several of these videos. Several of the videos feature the song, particularly the ones focused on mixing. For more about Letta and her music, check out the link in Fig. A-2.

Figure A-2. Letta QR code

Media

1. **The Skylight Interface.** In this video I walk through an overview of the SONAR Skylight user interface.
2. **Audio Device Setup.** Learn how to set up an audio interface in SONAR. I use examples of both Roland and third-party interfaces.
3. **MIDI Keyboard Controller Setup.** See how to configure a keyboard in this walkthrough, using the Roland A-500Pro MIDI Keyboard Controller.
4. **Working with Tracks and Clips.** Learn the basics for working in the SONAR Track view.
5. **The Control Bar.** Learn how to use the Control Bar, along with an explanation of the most used Control Bar modules.
6. **Smart Tool Editing.** Watch this concise demonstration to learn the key ways to use the Smart tool for audio editing.
7. **Intro to AudioSnap.** Learn how to correct timing of audio tracks by using the SONAR AudioSnap feature.

8. **Intro to Matrix View.** The Matrix view is a cool tool for mix and mash creativity. See how to load loops into the Matrix and record your performance back into the Track view.

9. **Automation Fundamentals.** This is an introduction to automating your faders and other parameters, to give your mix more life.

10. **Mix Example Part 1.** In this example I go over the setup for the mix of Letta's tune "Hold My Hand." Learn how I set up the track colors, track folders, buses, and master effects.

11. **Mix Example Part 2.** In this video, hear how I use ProChannel and insert effects on the vocals and drums. Finally, I go over the processing on the Master bus and then export the mix.

12. **Setting up a FaderPort.** The PreSonus Faderport is a very handy controller for work in SONAR. The setup is a bit tricky so I walk through it step by step.

Web Links by Figure Number

Web links in this book are presented as QR codes in figures. This makes it easy to link to the page by using any QR code reader app on your mobile device. This section is a cross-reference to the full web URL for each QR code figure in the book.

Figure 2.1. The Cakewalk Store
http://store.cakewalk.com

Figure 2.2. Cakewalk SONAR X2 Installation Instructions
http://www.cakewalk.com/support/kb/pages/x2_download_installation_instructions.aspx

Figure 2.6. Focusrite Windows Optimization
http://www.focusrite.com/answerbase/en/article.php?id=1071

Figure 2.7. Windows Optimization Cakewalk Forum
http://forum.cakewalk.com/tm.aspx?&m=1862515&mpage=1

Figure 2.8. Sweetwater Windows Optimization Tips
http://www.sweetwater.com/sweetcare/mac-pc-optimization/

Figure 2.9. Gearslutz DAW Building Thread
http://www.gearslutz.com/board/music-computers/560019-today-we-build-our-studio-pc-thread.html

Figure 2.10. Tom's Hardware DAW Building Thread
http://www.tomshardware.com/forum/353758-31-building-music-creation-production

Figure 2.11. Rain Computers
http://raincomputers.com

Figure 2.12. PCAudioLabs
http://pcaudiolabs.com

Figure 2.13. Purrrfect Audio
http://www.studiocat.com

Figure 2.14. ADK Pro Audio
http://adkproaudio.com

Figure 2.15. Sweetwater Sound
http://www.sweetwater.com/creation_station

Figure 2.16. Siber Systems GoodSync
http://www.goodsync.com

Figure 2.17. EaseUS Todo Backup Free
http://www.todo-backup.com/products/home/free-backup-software.htm

Figure 2.18. Dropbox
https://www.dropbox.com/

Figure 2.19. Agilebits 1Password
https://agilebits.com/onepassword/win
Figure 2.20. Microsoft Security Essentials
http://windows.microsoft.com/en-US/windows/products/security-essentials
Figure 3.1. Roland Drivers
http://www.rolandus.com/support/updates_driver
Figure 4.1. Roland Keyboard Drivers
http://www.roland.com/support/byproduct/plist.cfm?k=c&q=0000000883
Figure 5.18. SONAR X2 Online Help
http://www.cakewalk.com/documentation/
Figure 5.19. SONAR X2 PDF Reference Guide
http://www.cakewalk.com/Support/kb/reader.aspx/2007013290
Figure A.2. Letta's Homepage
www.Lettamusic.com

Index

quick **PRO**
guides *series*

Ableton Grooves
by Josh Bess
Softcover w/DVD-ROM •
978-1-4803-4574-4 • $19.99

**Producing Music
with Ableton Live**
by Jake Perrine
Softcover w/DVD-ROM •
978-1-4584-0036-9 • $16.99

**Sound Design,
Mixing, and
Mastering with
Ableton Live**
by Jake Perrine
Softcover w/DVD-ROM •
978-1-4584-0037-6 • $16.99

**Mastering
Auto-Tune**
by Max Mobley
Softcover w/ DVD-ROM •
978-1-4768-1417-9 • $16.99

**The Power in
Cakewalk SONAR**
by William Edstrom, Jr.
Softcover w/DVD-ROM •
978-1-4768-0601-3 • $16.99

**Mixing and
Mastering
with Cubase**
by Matthew Loel T. Hepworth
Softcover w/DVD-ROM •
978-1-4584-1367-3 • $16.99

**The Power
in Cubase:
Tracking Audio,
MIDI, and Virtual
Instruments**
by Matthew Loel T. Hepworth
Softcover w/DVD-ROM •
978-1-4584-1366-6 • $16.99

**Digital Performer
for Engineers and
Producers**
by David E. Roberts
Softcover w/DVD-ROM •
978-1-4584-0224-0 • $16.99

**The Power in
Digital Performer**
by David E. Roberts
Softcover w/DVD-ROM •
978-1-4768-1514-5 • $16.99

**Logic Pro for
Recording
Engineers
and Producers**
by Dot Bustelo
Softcover w/DVD-ROM •
978-1-4584-1420-5 • $16.99

**The Power in
Logic Pro:
Songwriting,
Composing,
Remixing, and
Making Beats**
by Dot Bustelo
Softcover w/DVD-ROM •
978-1-4584-1419-9 • $16.99

Musical iPad
*by Thomas Rudolph and
Vincent Leonard*
Softcover w/DVD-ROM •
978-1-4803-4244-6 • $19.99

**Mixing and
Mastering
with Pro Tools**
by Glenn Lorbecki
Softcover w/DVD-ROM •
978-1-4584-0033-8 • $16.99

**Tracking
Instruments
and Vocals with
Pro Tools**
by Glenn Lorbecki
Softcover w/DVD-ROM •
978-1-4584-0034-5 •$16.99

**The Power
in Reason**
by Andrew Eisele
Softcover w/DVD-ROM •
978-1-4584-0228-8 • $16.99

**Sound Design and
Mixing in Reason**
by Andrew Eisele
Softcover w/DVD-ROM •
978-1-4584-0229-5 • $16.99

**Studio One for
Engineers and
Producers**
by William Edstrom, Jr.
Softcover w/DVD-ROM •
978-1-4768-0602-0 • $16.99

HAL•LEONARD®

quickproguides.halleonardbooks.com
Prices, contents, and availability subject to change without notice.

0813